The Healing Mind

———————✳———————

The
Healing Mind

———————————✳———————————

Your Guide to the Power of
Meditation, Prayer, and Reflection

Eileen F. Oster

Foreword by Lesley Bradford, M.D.

PRIMA PUBLISHING

PRIMA PUBLISHING and colophon are trademarks of Prima Communications, Inc.

Illustrations by Jon Squitieri

Library of Congress Cataloging-in-Publication Data
Oster, Eileen.
    The healing mind : your guide to the power of meditation, prayer, and reflection / by Eileen Oster
        p.   cm.
    Includes bibliographical references and index.
    ISBN 0-7615-0488-5
    1. Meditation.   2. Mental healing.   I. Title.
BL627.085   1996
291.4'3—dc20   95-2170
                                                                     CIP

96 97 98 99 00 HH 10 9 8 7 6 5 4 3 2 1
Printed in the United States of America

How to Order:

Single copies may be ordered from Prima Publishing, P.O. Box 1260BK, Rocklin, CA 95677; telephone (916) 632-4400. Quantity discounts are also available. On your letterhead, include information concerning the intended use of the books and the number of books you wish to purchase.

This book is dedicated to many who share in my life.

To my husband, Neill S. Oster, M.D., thank you for believing in the unconventional dreams and miracles of life.

To my family, which is quite large now, I thank you all for your roles in the creation of this work and the collective spiritual growth we all share, in pain or joy.

To all those souls—friends, patients, students, and challengers—who have touched my life and been my greatest teachers, I thank you.

And to the One Whom I Love with All My Heart and Soul— may we all continue to sound the song of love that resonates within and come home.

---★---

CONTENTS

✳

✳

✳

✳

CHAPTER NINE

Dreams, Visions, and Miracles   148

✳

CHAPTER TEN

The Life Cycle As a Sacred Journey   173

ACKNOWLEDGMENTS

There are many to whom acknowledgment must be given for the evolution of this work.

To Kathleen Oitzinger, Ph.D., my mentor and friend, I thank you for all the years of psychotherapeutic training and love.

To Reverend Rosalyn L. Bruyere, my healing teacher, may your work always be honored.

My sincerest thanks to Lesley Bradford, M.D., who wrote the lovely foreword to this book on extremely short notice and with much graciousness.

My deep appreciation to Joseph Sciabbarrasi, M.D., who shared his valuable time and knowledge to read and comment on the contents of this book.

To Reverend Susan Brown my gratitude for sharing your resources and support.

To Reverend Susan Lovett my thanks for all your assistance and compassion.

I am ever grateful to Janice Gillis, who painstakingly typed this manuscript from my longhand writing.

My gratitude to Kathy Amorosa, for her editorial assistance prior to publisher submission.

To a young illustrator, Jon Squitieri, your grandfather is very proud.

To Margaret Russell, my literary agent and human angel, I say thank you for believing in this book.

And last, but not least, my gratitude to Georgia Hughes, Susan Silva, Lisa Armstrong, and Rachel Myers, my editors at Prima Publishing, who allowed this book to become a physical reality.

FOREWORD

This book outlines a way for the reader to have a deeper, more meaningful relationship to his or her own life process. Our technological world often leaves us feeling disconnected from others and ourselves. Psychotherapies have been able to fill only a portion of the void we feel within. As we struggle to combat our illnesses and to achieve our full potential, we need both a vision of what is possible, and guidelines for how to achieve it. That is what this book provides. The author presents a perspective on the purpose of life, and a way of practicing spiritual disciplines that lead one toward a sense of connectedness with the Mystery of Life. Further, she demonstrates how spiritual practice can be integrated into one's daily life, how there is, in fact, no split between the spiritual and the practical, between energy and matter, between our inner and outer life. This is a book about becoming whole.

A culture's philosophy and values are reflected in its institutions. Change occurs more slowly in government than it does at the grassroots level, but in a democracy it does eventually respond. This is reflected today in the American health-care system, which has been dominated throughout this century by Western allopathic medicine. Like the rest of the American culture, medicine has become increasingly technological; specialization and super-specialization have become necessary in order to keep up with these advances, and escalating costs have led to third-party payors controlling the dispensation of medical care. Patients complain about being depersonalized in this system. At the same time, a grassroots movement has emerged, commonly known as "holistic," "alternative," or "complementary" medicine. Many of its therapeutic modalities antedate Western medicine by hundreds, if not thousands, of years, and are actually traditional healing techniques. They include massage, relaxation, acupuncture, diet, herbs, chiropractic, yoga, energy, and shamanism, among others.

These two health-care systems have been functioning separately from one another; practitioners and consumers of each system have tended to view the other with mistrust and suspicion. At the root of this lies an ideological barrier. Conventional medicine reflects Western scientific thinking, which is mechanistic and materialistic in its study of man from the point of view of anatomy, physiology and biochemistry. Many alternative therapies derive from Eastern or native traditions which hold a more spiritual view of man, and posit an energy field around and within the human body. Unfortunately, healers have allied themselves with one camp or the other, with little or no dialogue between them. Research indicates that 34 percent of the U.S. population uses alternative therapies; of those combining conventional and alternative therapy, 72 percent do not inform their medical doctors of their use of nonconventional methods.

In 1992 an event took place which was as significant for Western medicine as the falling of the Berlin Wall in the world political arena: the United States Congress mandated the formation of the National Institutes of Health Office of Alternative Medicine. The purposes of this office are to investigate, evaluate and validate "alternative" interventions, provide a database and clearinghouse for information on these modalities, and to train researchers and conduct scientific research in alternative medicine. This is a signal to me that a new era of dialogue has indeed begun. As we bring to alternative therapies the light of scientific research, we all stand to benefit. This is no small task, as the methodology which is used by conventional medicine cannot be applied to some alternative therapies; new methodology will have to be devised.

In any discussion of research, one's terms need to be defined. The word "healing" has been problematic for me. To heal means "to make whole or sound; restore health; free from ailment." After 20 years of practicing medicine, first as a family physician, then as a psychiatrist, I have had to reconcile myself with the fact that there is very little that medicine actually cures. We can prolong life with transplants, replace joints, reduce fever and inflammation, bypass clogged arteries, block gastric acid secretion, replace insulin and other hormones, but in most cases we do not heal the underlying disease process. Despite the marvels of technology, vaccinations and hygiene have had the most profound of all influences on the course of disease in human history. Even antibiotics are being outsmarted today by mutating bacteria. And patients' responses to our very best interventions vary. As with infectious diseases, characteristics of the host or patient have an enormous impact on the course of an illness. The state of an organism with respect to nutrition, rest, stress, level of activity, mental attitude, emotional condition, and psychosocial support are all known to influence that organism's ability to deal with disease-causing factors. We can kill tumor cells, but often the cancer reappears later. In anaclitic depression, babies who are provided with a safe, clean environment and adequate diet, but denied human contact, actually die. Then there is the infamous placebo response: inactive preparations achieve responses as though they were active ingredients. The "mind-body connection" is no longer theory; we know it to be fact.

Healing is a complex process involving the interaction of many factors. Now that I understand this, I cannot maintain the grandiose notion that I alone can heal another. The best we can do is to stimulate and support those factors which will alleviate suffering and help another move toward wholeness. If I conceive of man as a physical body, my interventions will be mechanical and chemical; this has been the main focus of conventional medicine. But if I conceive of man as physical and spiritual/energetic, my interventions will extend to include his soul: this is the focus of many alternative therapies. I believe that we need both.

It is perhaps no coincidence that at the same time in history the wall between East and West has come down, quantum physics tells us that matter is also energy, and conventional medicine discovers the mind-body connection. This book is very timely. Not only do ancient spiritual traditions tell us to meditate, self-examine and pray, modern research shows that meditating lowers blood pressure, and prayer can affect a host of cellular processes from bacterial mutations to the firing rate of pacemaker cells. The use of visualization can warm the extremities, there is such a thing as ESP, and therapeutic touch can enhance the immune system. The implications of this book for modern medicine are enormous.

Research may or may not validate the exact energy model presented here. No research has shown the existence of structural identities called id, ego and superego. Yet out of Freud's model of the human psyche has grown a specialty within conventional medicine which has helped many achieve greater wholeness. "Psychic healing" may in some hands be quackery, but in others it is a useful adjunct to conventional methods of diagnosis and treatment as illustrated herein. I welcome the coming of the day when, instead of alternative versus conventional medicine, we have integrated health care for the whole person.

To the adherent practitioner of conventional medicine, I would say: let's do the research and see what the data shows. A third of your patients are utilizing alternative medicine. Far better that you educate yourself about the techniques and communicate with these patients and their healers than to turn a blind eye to them. Remember, Copernicus was scorned for his suggestion that the sun, not the earth, is at the center of our solar system.

To the advocate of alternative medicine, I would say: be patient with skeptics. Honor the scientific method and participate in it. Be willing to subject your practices to scrutiny. We all need to know what exactly it is that you are doing which achieves results, and whether they are reproducible results.

To both I would say: do not let attachment to your ideology blind you to either the data or the possibilities. Personal experience has taught me that collaborative work with healers from other disciplines not only improves the quality of care our patients receive, but enhances our wholeness as well.

To the student I would say: pay attention to the word discipline, for that is the basis of the spiritual life. This is neither play nor a formula for instant gratification. It is practice, just like playing scales on a piano. It is learning to use your instrument in a new way. There is a vibratory component to the human being; even plants grow better when exposed to certain kinds of music.

Meditation, self-examination and prayer are forms of technology for sensing and affecting the vibrations of your being, and of those around you. You need not abandon your religious belief system, or even have one, in order to use these methods. See what experiences your spiritual practice produces. They may not be the same as the author's. Or you may label them differently. That which she calls "spirit guide" you may call "the Holy Spirit" or "intuition." Labels are not important; what is important is that you have the experiences. Let your belief system grow out of them, for this is the path of the mystic. And discover what music your instrument can play as it becomes more finely tuned.

Much suffering is, I believe, the result of disconnecting from our inner experience. It is this connection that the techniques of meditation, self-examination, and prayer repair. They are, indeed, the tools of the healing mind.

LESLEY BRADFORD, M.D.

Chapter 1

✳

LIFE'S PURPOSE

What is the purpose of life? The answer to this question is highly subjective. There are many religious and nonreligious ideas about life's purpose. The view set forth in this book is clearly a spiritual one. It is neither new nor unique. But it is simple and basic. Life is an opportunity to evolve the soul. It is a gift whereby we can come to know ourselves, fulfill our heartfelt dreams and desires, know love, and experience divinity. It is a beginning and a return. The soul enters a physical body and begins the journey of human life to return to the journey of spirit life. Enriched, erudite, and God-connected, the soul emerges from the physical body and returns to an eternal realm of consciousness.

In honoring our self as an eternal being in human form we can look at the body, mind, spirit continuum through new eyes to heal the self and move toward finding and fulfilling our soul's purpose in this life's sojourn.

We (our souls) actually have two adventures here in life. One is the task of uncovering our true self and purpose and the other is finding our niche in the larger scope of humanity's purpose. When we honor the self, we learn to honor all the selves or people who surround us in life. When we find our soul's purpose, it is always joined to a larger reality. In uplifting our own self and spirit, we uplift the rest of humanity. Healing has a ripple effect. All are joined to the Divine.

This view of human life as part of the soul's journey has a depth and richness that many regard as heavy and intense. To those who wish to view life superficially as a quest to gather material goods and who live life as an avoidance of death, the view presented here *is* heavy and intense. This book is expressly written for those of us who have traveled life's path through trials and crises and come to the realization that there is more to life than scrambling for the next high, running the rat race of working at a job that has no personal meaning, or living a life prescribed for us by others.

Life has spiritual meaning, and human beings have need of each other. For those of us who have stood bereft and in desperation called to a higher power for help because we knew instinctively there was something we were missing and needed to find—it is here. The bridge of earth and spirit abides within each of us. The opportunity to awaken our consciousness and live life in a purposeful and spiritual way is realizable for us all. There is a way which can bring freedom from the past, peace in the present, and joy in the moment. It is a way that celebrates life, joins us in fellowship with one another, and honors the uniqueness of every being. The way is to know thyself through the processes of meditation, self-examination, and prayer.

These processes are surprisingly practical and sensible. Performed regularly, these spiritual disciplines can transform your life. They bring clarity, self-knowledge, and divine connection to spirit. Life becomes what you have always dreamed it could be— and more.

The place where you begin these spiritual disciplines is the most perfect place to start. There is no better place for you to be than where you are. This is the beauty of these spiritual practices. There is no penalty for starting late nor order of preference in initiating these practices. Many of us have some form of prayer life. Many of us self-examine to a degree, and some of us have attempted meditation.

Whatever the order begun, the practice initiated, or the level of expertise, the goal remains the same—finding self and finding peace.

Within the pages of this book you will find the word "God." It is used for simplicity. If you find yourself more comfortable with another word, use it. The only concept that is important is that there is a divine power greater than yourself. I choose to call that power God. Many find the term Higher Power preferable, and that's just fine. We are absolutely Higher-Powered!

Life's purpose has a direct connection to God. The process of life demands that in finding yourself, you find God. Truly, God exists within you and you are a part of God. This idea may be hard to swallow for many, but it is not the purpose of this book to present only ideas that are easy. Life is not easy. There are hills and valleys and miracles. If we take our Higher Power with us into the valleys, we will most assuredly benefit from the depths. That is why developing spiritual disciplines is essential. When practiced regularly they become a foundation you can rely on. Even in the darkest moments of despair, your voice is heard and an answer will surely follow. If you have a strong spiritual foundation you will always be able to get through the tough times and emerge stronger and more deeply loved.

If the purpose of life is to evolve the soul, then it follows that we will go through experiences in life from which we learn and grow. To do so, we need tools that provide us with fortitude and insight. Unfortunately, too few of us are properly prepared for our life journeys. We often stumble along with no clear picture of who we are and what our individual passion or purpose in life is. For each person there is an undeniable individual purpose in being. How does one find it? I propose that meditation, self-examination, and prayer are the tools through which we find ourselves.

In finding ourselves, we can find our connection to other people and build a life which is personally fulfilling and meaningful. To know ourselves in relation to all things is clear perception. To come to know ourselves is an ongoing and continual process, as is living. We forever grow and develop. To do so in an articulate and authentic manner is inspirational to others. Those who have become impeccable at living life become our spiritual teachers.

If this text thus far appears lofty and highly philosophical, it is only because that's the way life itself is. In all my work in this world as a human being and as an occupational therapist, I have found people from every walk of life to be profound. I believe in the sagaciousness and depth of each soul because of my experiences here on earth. I have the great privilege of meeting people at the most vulnerable points in their lives. Be it a medical crisis, a psychological or emotional crisis, or a spiritual crisis, people are capable of great spiritual acumen and awareness. What we all need in these critical moments is to know that we are not alone and to realize that another soul sees us and recognizes our need to be validated and heard. The simple act of truly touching another being is enough to make the heavens hush.

The most powerful place on earth is where one sees the need of another as no different from one's own need. We each need to feel connected to one another and to uplift the consciousness of all souls through our living.

A divinely-inspired spiritual fellowship shares the belief that we are all the same, that, each of us hungers for the same goals—love, oneness, and connection. These are the gifts we can share with one another when we have them for ourselves.

Meditation, self-examination, and prayer are the ways by which we can achieve a sense of oneness, connection, and love. We can make the most of this human lifetime, if we so choose, by learning these spiritual practices. These practices have been taught by all the beloved masters of every spiritual path on earth.

The Physical Body: Does It Join in Life's Purpose?

The body is part of the purpose of life. For what vessel contains the soul at this stage of its spritual journey? The physical body. There is an explosion of information available now that speaks of the mind-body connection and the roles the body, mind, and spirit play in relation to one another. Precisely because this book addresses the healing powers of meditation, self-examination, and prayer, I would be remiss not to include the physical body as a part of the whole in this work. However, as a responsible healer and health professional, I must state at the outset that there is no magic formula for healing the body. There is a simple explanation for this incredibly complex problem. The body is temporary. It is not a permanent residence of the self, the spirit, or the soul. It is merely a temporary teaching tool in which we may or may not evolve the soul. This is in no way meant to demean the significance of living on the material plane in a physical body. There are wondrous and powerful experiences to have in physical form, and who among us does not wish for a lifetime of robust physical health and comfort and a death that is painless and accomplished at an age considered appropriate? We all wish for such a life. I wish I could say that if you meditate ten times daily, self-examine a minimum of three times daily, and pray as necessary, you will have a perfectly healthy body and leave when you are ready. Sorry, it just isn't so. You can do all the right things and still get sick or need surgery or have an accident.

So, what's the point of all this body, mind, and spirit medicine if it's not a sure thing? It is a sure thing. Personal healing is an intimate journey to evolve the self. There are most certainly things we can do and practice that afford the physical body the best opportunities to heal, preventive measures we can take to avoid behaviors that are destructive to the body, and spiritual practices we can adopt that are enormously beneficial and nurturing to the body. Traditional western medicine would not exist if the body wasn't considered important enough to try to heal and care for. Alternative and eastern medicine techniques and practices also consider healing the physical body as relevant and important.

My concern here—and it is shared by other responsible individuals in this field—is that our physical health or illness not be a measure of our spiritual development. Many in the mind-body movement too easily assign blame to themselves for becoming ill. They weren't doing something right or they did something really wrong and are paying the consequences. We must refrain from judging ourselves so harshly or judging others in this vein. The manifestation of spirit, and each person's journey through this lifetime, is unique and special. We must learn to regard the cycle of physical life for what it is in all its glory and pain. It is a cycle. Life is a moment on the space-time continuum through which we pass with the express purpose of evolving and assisting others to evolve. As a healer I am absolutely devoted to caring for sick and well bodies. I will always strive to heal whatever ails, and that includes the body. We shall always try to maintain health through all the means available to us. There are means to maintain health, recover health, and heal illnesses. We need to remember that there are also means to comfort the dying and that death and physical illness are not failures, but perhaps are greater miracles to those who journey to them than a healthy person will ever know. Illness is a part of life and we do not understand all the workings of divine spirit or the mystery revealed for each personal spiritual quest.

Some spiritual systems teach that the body is so unimportant that it can be disregarded and uncared for because it is of no essential importance in spiritual life.

But the body has a major role as a spiritual vehicle for the soul's evolution. Many people do not even consider their spiritual self of significance until faced with a body that has become diseased, injured, or unruly.

I believe there is a balance between the physical and the spritual life. For ultimately, though the physical body ceases to be a part of who we are, at this point in the space-time continuum it is joined with us and houses our very nature. It is the temple for our soul's growth and is imbued with spiritual essence or "life force" energy while our soul resides in it. Because of this, our bodies can be a source of supreme, spirited life force energy that can benefit ourselves and others on many planes or levels, including the physical plane.

All spiritual self-discovery can be viewed as miraculous, and the physical body is an energetic part of who we are at this moment. There are countless stories of miraculous physical healings associated with meditation, self-examination, and prayer. There are also miraculous emotional and spiritual healings associated with these practices.

Meditation, Self-Examination, and Prayer

Meditation, self-examination, and prayer practiced in an ongoing and consistent way will transform the person who uses them. Too often the spiritual life is looked upon as lacking real power in the material world. Nothing could be farther from the truth. Many times people think that if they "get spiritual" they will have to give up those things that make them feel powerful or successful in the world. This is not the real truth. In becoming spiritual, we find out what is important and what is not. Frequently, what we held as significant loses its significance and other beliefs fill the void.

The duty of the spiritual person is to walk upon the earth with real power and manifest that power in accordance with spirit. There is no set rule or regulation about what a person has to do or be in the world when he or she becomes spiritual. If it is your heart's desire to be a librarian, a corporate executive, or a health-care provider, then you can be the most exceptional example of whichever you choose. If you desire to be a mother or father, then you can be the most devoted and nurturing parent in the world. There are no limitations in spirituality, only possibilities. For those who have lost everything and are starting anew, there are only endless opportunities.

When people practice meditation, self-examination, and prayer, they are not becoming perfect. They are committed to learning a way that will bring them closer to living a life that is functional, more free, and more loving. This way is powerful. When people become proficient at self-knowing, listening for guidance, and prayer, they become extremely powerful. There are few who would approach a centered and focused human being without regard. Being spiritual does not imply weakness. Rather, it bestows great reserves of strength, which others seek.

A world where people are free to choose how they live does not make for a peaceful, safe environment. There are many levels of consciousness, and many people do not choose to live a spiritual or God-directed life. The spiritual practitioner has need of the gifts of clarity, good judgment, and Higher Power awareness that come from the disciplines of meditation, self-examination, and prayer.

As stated before, these disciplines are immensely practical and sensible. Who would not revel in a life in which clear guidance and insight were the regular course of the day? Pitfalls could be spotted, healthy choices made, and experiences that benefit the soul illuminated. Such a life is the result of meditation, self-examination, and prayer. The more diligently these are practiced, the larger and more efficient the reward.

Each day, time should be allotted for meditation, self-examination, and prayer. This becomes the framework by which one lives the day. Consistency and scheduling may vary, but effort and willingness are crucial. If you fail to keep a spiritual discipline this day, you can begin again tomorrow. The cumulative effect of attempting and doing will always be positive. Nothing is ever lost in spiritual practice but time, and time is always *now* in spiritual life.

Learning occurs through the process of doing these spiritual disciplines. Even those of us who toil diligently along this path will have times when we forget. The wonderful aspect of spiritual practice is that you can remember at any moment and begin again.

I have known many people who feel it is necessary to leave their "regular" life and retreat to a religious or spiritual center to learn the disciplines explored in this book. In actuality, we can learn these practices in the course of our everyday lives and retreat if necessary on our vacations to immerse ourselves in a less stressful and more peaceful environment.

It is my goal to be able to bring these practices into my daily life and use them for the purposes for which they are intended. Under stressful circumstances we are challenged to grow. There is positive stress and negative stress, and stressful circumstances offer us the opportunity to rise to the occasion and create peace for ourselves amidst the storm. Even if you are juggling work, family obligations, and chores, you are perfectly suited to practicing these principles. Propitiously, they are designed for use in the "real world."

The processes of meditation, self-examination, and prayer will be explored in the following chapters. These nondenominational, nonreligious processes are a part of what is now known as the new age of spirituality. Perhaps there is a new dawning of ancient metaphysical constructs that have been with us through the ages, but to categorize it as "new age" has become a way of reducing what these spiritual metaphysical constructs are and of lumping together many beliefs or theories under one name that can be trivialized and mocked. Therefore, I refrain from using this term throughout this book. There is nothing trivial about healing. An open mind and willingness to learn will go a long way in beginning these practices.

Chapter 2

✳

MEDITATION

Meditation is a state of consciousness that differs from the state of consciousness with which we usually interact with the world. It has been described by many as a state of heightened awareness of all senses, a state in which peace and comfort envelop the individual who is meditating, a state of calm serenity that offers repose from the hustle and bustle of daily life.

Meditation is all of these things and more. There are many levels of meditation. The goal of meditation is inner peace through connection to one's self and the Divine Spirit. Much can be revealed through the practice of meditation. Many answers to one's struggles can be found in meditation. Worlds of spirit reside in the altered state of expanded awareness. Access to eternal knowledge and wisdom come through the practice of meditation.

This sounds good. So why is it so difficult to learn meditation? For the beginner, the most challenging aspect is learning how to still the mind long enough to enter into a truly meditative state. Out comes the unending laundry list of daily activities, worries, problems, and various other things one should be doing. And since the beginner has not yet transcended the talkative mind and discovered the quiet mind, he has no reference point for where he is attempting to go. Thankfully, there is a solution to this problem, and techniques can be learned that will help the initiate enter into a state of meditation.

First an error needs to be corrected. Many people continue to promulgate the myth that meditation is an entrance into a state of "nothingness." This idea alone can cause the mind to rebel. How does one enter into "nothingness?" I haven't a clue because my experience of meditation has always been to enter a state of fullness of being. There is nothing "nothing" about it. Perhaps what was meant by the sages of old is that we leave the world of noise and enter a world of quiet where unlimited and unbounded thought awaits us. We enter the "sea of true mind" where all previously held ego constraints leave us. This place is unfamiliar at first, and then, always known.

Perhaps "nothingness" is a misinterpretation of a state which is known as "beginner's mind." Beginner's mind or "the empty bowl" theory posits a willingness to give up all limited thought and enter into meditation as an innocent ready to discover what awaits there. I shall always hope for beginner's mind, for when we can successfully achieve it, we are, paradoxically, not beginners.

Meditation is a spiritual practice. Its benefits to the body, the emotions, and the mind are measurable to a degree. It is well-known that meditation can decrease blood pressure, reduce heart rate and respiration, and increase alpha brain waves, which are beneficial to the body and associated with relaxed wakefulness. The medical community regards meditation as a form of stress reduction that has positive physiological effects.

The emotional advantages of meditation are evident as well. People who meditate regularly learn to bring their emotions into balance. Those who are ruled by emotion can learn to temper their responses and to allow their emotions a proper position in their lives, and those who suppress emotion can learn to allow their emotions expression and to give them a rightful place in their lives.

The mind also benefits from the practice of meditation. Meditation broadens the mind and enables the meditator to absorb more information with less expenditure of energy. As acuity and clarity develop, the results of regular meditation become evident to the practitioner.

The individual who pursues meditation as a spiritual practice will open a channel within to the world of higher consciousness. This connection brings inner peace and greater joys than have ever been experienced before.

Here is where the spiritual practice leaves most of modern medicine behind: the world of spirit and personal connection to divinity is not measurable by scientific devices.

Life Force

A few basic concepts must be explained in order to grasp meditation as a real physical, psychological, and spiritual discipline.

Life force or *qi* (pronounced *chi*) is the energy that all living beings possess and to which they have access. Most people are aware of the ebb and flow of their life force. We have times of great energy and strength and times of depletion and depression. We feel these changes physically, emotionally, and spiritually. Often, we relate our energy fluctuations to situations in life and our reactions to them. If we are feeling good and positive, we can go through difficult circumstances with ease. When we are down or overwhelmed, ordinary life tasks can appear monumental and exhausting.

Qi is a power within us which directly relates to our state of physical, emotional, and spiritual health. The mind or will possesses life force and energy that we can direct to carry out our desires. Much, both positive and negative, has been accomplished by will. Life force is an energy that encompasses our entire being, and with an understanding of it, we can procure and use it to improve our health and to fulfill our destiny as magnificent bearers of light.

Meditation involves life force. In full meditation one incorporates the physical body, the emotional body, the mind, and the spiritual body. (I use the word "body," in reference to emotion and spirit, to describe the energetic states that reside within each individual. These are discussed more fully later.) When we sit to meditate, we bring with us our entire self and incorporate all parts of ourselves in meditation.

The physical body is often neglected by those who teach meditation because it is not seen as "spiritual." But the physical body hungers for sustenance and spirit as much as the rest of us, and when infused with spirited life force, the body becomes a vehicle for our work in this world. It can be in union with our life's purpose and it certainly is the container for the soul at this time. The sweetness of a physical touch powered by love and compassion is healing. We are physical beings and can learn to direct our physicality in healthy and functional ways. Frequently we feel that our physical bodies betray us in their addictions, diseases, and lack of perfection. But, our physical bodies are a part of the whole and require our attention. The physical body must be included in life's purpose.

Conceptualizing Life Force

I am going to describe several ideas, which may be new to you. They are not scientifically proven at this point in time. Medical science does not yet have tools to fully measure the energy that I am here calling life force although research is currently underway in this area, which is known as the human energy field or biofield theory.

Great strides are being made in western medicine to investigate what is termed "alternative medicine." The National Institute of Health has established an Office of Alternative Medicine whose primary purpose is to evaluate alternative medical treatments. In response to the inescapable fact that so many Americans are using alternative medicine therapies, the traditional medical community has begun to cooperate with members of the alternative medical community. Even in light of this breakthrough, mountains of research and investigation remain to be explored before western science can ascertain "scientific truths" regarding any form of these alternative medical practices.

Meditation is considered an alternative medicine practice. Life force or *qi* theories are derived from eastern medicine, metaphysical, and mystical traditions.

The concepts of life force, energy fields, the human aura, and the chakra system all view the human body as more than just an anatomical and physiological arrangement of visible parts, such as the circulatory, digestive, nervous, or skeletal systems. The life force or energy field theory purports that in addition to traditional anatomy and physiology there is a system of "energy." This system serves as the template of our physical bodies and is, in fact, a foundation for our physical existence. The life force is as essential to our living physical bodies as breath is to human life.

Although the concepts of life force I am about to share with you are not scientific fact, it would be well to remember at this point that love is not scientifically provable, either. We know it exists because most humans feel it does. But love is not measurable by any scientific device. It is experienced. This is a good personal barometer for the existence of life force. Can you experience it?

The following ideas are known in metaphysical circles and mystical tradition. I offer them to you as a means of assisting you in your meditation efforts. It is essential to have a basic understanding of energy and life force to gain optimal results in meditation. Therefore, in the spirit of open-mindedness, I invite you to listen to a system of thought rooted in mysticism.

There exists a primary line of light, or life force line, through the human body that is understood by mystics as energetically connecting us to the Divine Source—God. This projection of light radiates in a vertical line through the center or crown of the head, courses in a straight line centrally through the body, and exits the lower body between the legs to extend into the earth. This core line of light differs from the chakra system (Figures 1 and 2), although the life force line and the chakras are confluent. The chakras form a system within the human body that gathers energy from the earth, circulates that energy through our mind-body system and organizes physical, emotional, mental, and spiritual energy. In contrast, the life force line contains the more permanent soul.

The following three diagrams represent a conceptual view of both the chakra system and the life force line within the framework of the human body (Figures 1, 2, and 3).

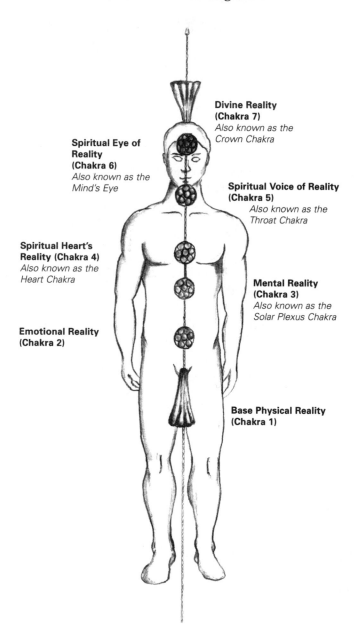

**Divine Reality
(Chakra 7)**
*Also known as the
Crown Chakra*

**Spiritual Eye of
Reality
(Chakra 6)**
*Also known as the
Mind's Eye*

**Spiritual Voice of Reality
(Chakra 5)**
*Also known as the
Throat Chakra*

**Spiritual Heart's
Reality (Chakra 4)**
*Also known as the
Heart Chakra*

**Mental Reality
(Chakra 3)**
*Also known as the
Solar Plexus Chakra*

**Emotional Reality
(Chakra 2)**

**Base Physical Reality
(Chakra 1)**

Figure 1   Anterior View of the Chakra System

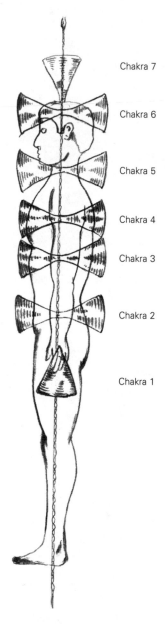

Chakra 7

Chakra 6

Chakra 5

Chakra 4

Chakra 3

Chakra 2

Chakra 1

Figure 2 Lateral View of the Chakra System

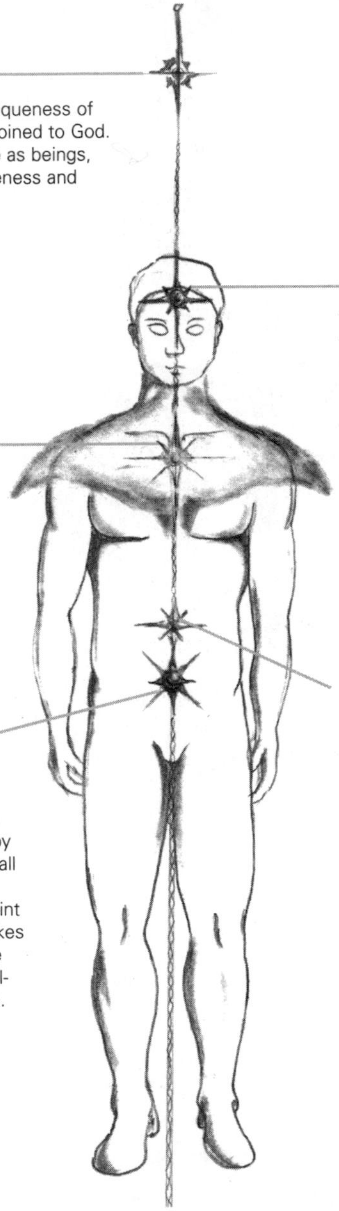

Star of Uniqueness
This point represents our uniqueness of being as both separate and joined to God. We were given life to evolve as beings, and it is here that our uniqueness and oneness are birthed.

Gate of Entrance
This opening on the life force line represents our entranceway to the eternal. It is located at the points of connection between the third-eye chakras and the base-of-the-crown chakra. Anatomic location in the brain would be the diencephalon area including the thalamus, hypothalamus, pituitary, and pineal glands. Through this gate we can mindfully enter the life force line and know our relationship to God.

Seat of the Soul
This area encompasses the chest in the human body. It is where the longing and desires of the soul reside. If you have ever felt a heart's longing or a profound pull towards spirit, you most likely feel it here. When people experience loss or sadness, they frequently experience a heaviness in this area.

Tan Tien
This is the balance point of connection for us in relation to the earth. In physiotherapy or movement science, we call it the center of gravity. Tan Tien is a representational point around which movement takes place in martial arts. It is the point for our human physical-soul connection to the earth.

Central Star of Being
This central point, located near and above the umbilicus area and deep within our life force line, represents our essence of being. It is our center of light, the point from which our whole body and being can radiate out like a star in the world.

Figure 3 Anterior View of Primary Line of Light or Life Force Line

The Chakra System

Chakra is a Sanskrit word meaning "wheel of light." These seven wheels (diagrammed in Figures 1 and 2) are actually energy vortexes of light, vibration, sound, and color that function together in a human energy field system to circulate and organize energy within the body, mind, and spirit continuum. Each chakra performs specific functions and also works with all the chakras to gather and move energy through the body. The chakra system exists on the physical level as well as on other energy levels to bridge the energetic consciousness from the base physical reality (chakra 1), to the emotional reality (chakra 2), to the mental reality (chakra 3), to the spiritual heart's reality (chakra 4), to the spiritual voice of reality (chakra 5), to the spiritual eye of reality (chakra 6), to the divine reality (chakra 7).

I will not go further in my explanation of the chakra system at this time because the meditations and exercises I include in this chapter deal primarily with the life force line which, as previously mentioned, is present at a different energetic level than the chakra system, although the two are confluent. In a later chapter, I will further discuss the chakra system.

For an in-depth understanding of the chakra system, I refer you to the Reverend Rosalyn L. Bruyeres' excellent series on the chakra system, *Wheels of Light*. Reverend Bruyere sits on the Alternative Medicine Committee Board at the National Institute of Health as an expert on human energy fields and spiritual healing. She is one of the foremost teachers in this field.

The Primary Line of Light or Life Force Line

The primary line of light contains five points or concentrations of life force which represent the following:

> TAN TIEN   This is the balance point that connects our human physical soul to the earth. Located in the pelvic bowl area, this is the point around which movement takes place. In physiotherapy or movement science, it is called the body's center of gravity. In martial arts, it is know as the tan tien.

CENTRAL STAR OF BEING   This central point, located near and above the umbilicus area and deep within our life force line, represents our essence of being. It is our center of light, the point from which our whole body and being can radiate out like a star in the world.

SEAT OF THE SOUL   This area encompasses the chest in the human body. It is where the longing and desires of the soul reside. If you have ever felt a heart's longing or a profound pull toward spirit, you most likely felt it here. When people experience loss or sadness, they frequently experience a heaviness in this area.

GATE OF ENTRANCE   This opening on the life force line represents our mind's entranceway to the eternal. It is located at the points of connection between the third eye chakras and the base of the crown chakra. The anatomic location in the brain corresponds to the diencephalon area, which includes the thalamus, hypothalamus, pituitary, and pineal glands. Through this gate we can mindfully enter the life force line and know our relationship to God.

STAR OF UNIQUENESS   This point represents our uniqueness as both separate and joined to God. We were given life to evolve as beings, and it is here that our uniqueness and oneness are birthed.

The life force line continues past the star of uniqueness to the one source of all life. Here is where we are all joined in oneness. It is my hope that in divine meditation you will be graced with the opportunity to experience the exalted state of consciously being connected to our highest source. The life force line accesses life force from above and below—we are literally the bridge between heaven and earth.

This basic explanation of the life force line or primary line of light is quite useful in facilitating energetic meditative states. Even if you do not believe in the actual existence of the life force line, you can envision it and employ the image of an energetic force of light ascending through your body to traverse symbolically from physical to divine nature. In meditation, whatever is comfortable for the individual is fine. Mystics don't often care what road you take to meditation; they are mostly concerned with the achievement of the meditative state.

Centering Life Force

You begin centering your life force by learning to ground your energy. As physical beings we derive physical energy from the elements and dynamics of the earth. Breath, movement, sound, and light are all qualities which we physical beings share with the earth. The earth moves; the earth breathes and resonates sound. It contains its own source of fire and light. Our bodies, too, require breath, movement, and light. Even our cells vibrate at a certain rate. By connecting consciously to the earth's energetic vibrations, we can center and ground our energy. This physical grounding and connection to the earth as our home is essential to obtaining the energy that magnifies our life force and allows for increased ease in entering a meditative state and accessing the physical *qi* we need to feed our cells.

Techniques for grounding or centering include movement, breathing, sounding, and inner light exercises. These techniques are ancient and widely used in many religions and cultures. In yoga, breath and movement are used; in churches around the world, singing, bells, and chanting are used; in Judaism, davening with prayer is common and on certain holy days the shofar sounds, calling the soul to awaken. Drumming and dance are essential parts of the rituals of many cultures. And around the world fire and candles, the sun, and the light of the stars represent the light within. The use of these techniques or practices to enter an altered state is universal. Breath, movement, sound, and light are fundamental to meditation.

Breathing is natural. In learning meditation breathing can become an obstacle, if focused on too obsessively. I have seen many people have great difficulty meditating, because they were consumed with whether they were or were not breathing correctly. Simply taking a few deep breaths to relax the body is quite enough to initiate meditation. Once relaxed, the body will naturally breathe in a comfortable manner and our thoughts may move on to other places.

There are myriad movements and positions used in meditation. Dance, tai chi, and yoga all provide movements and positions for meditation. I usually teach basic relaxation and grounding movements to facilitate learning meditation. First, gradually stretch and shake out your arms and legs and gently roll your neck from side to side to assist in relaxing and centering. Then use the following body positions to improve grounding: Stand with your feet shoulder width apart and bend your knees slightly. Rotate the pelvic girdle to find a center of stability and help ground your energy. After kinesthetically feeling your feet, legs, and pelvis connecting to terra firma, you can move into a comfortable seated posture in a chair or on a cushion. Keep your spine as upright and aligned as comfortably possible, and rest your hands, palms up, on your knees. Your head should be upright, looking forward.

The act of sounding is very difficult for people in our American culture. Making a vibrational noise seems tantamount to farting in public. If you can get past the shame issue of sounding, this practice is quite helpful in grounding and centering energy. It additionally shifts your energy field and begins to alter your consciousness. Rolling an "Om" out of your mouth and through your body feels good. *Ahh, Ehh, Eee, Ooo,* or *Uuu* clearly vibrated can be sensed through your entire body.

Once you are relaxed, positioned, and sounded, your mind can focus on light. Meditation can be done with eyes opened or closed. When teaching meditation initially I usually instruct students to close their eyes because it is easier to learn meditation this way. Closing your eyes to bring your attention inward allows your awareness to shift to inner sources of light and ultimately to the gate of light that bridges vision between the celestial and earthly worlds. This is commonly called the "third eye."

Clearing the Mind

The exercises of centering and grounding aid in clearing the mind. If, after centering, you still harbor intrusive thoughts that interfere with your meditation, practice this mental exercise. Stop resisting or pushing away these thoughts and just allow them to float by your mind's eye while acknowledging each one. Note the thoughts as they pass and affirm that you will be able to deliberate on them after your meditation. Once the list of thoughts is diminished, return to your center and ground once again. Breathe, relax, and focus your mind on the light within you.

Forms of Meditation

As mentioned previously, there are many forms of meditation. Common meditation techniques include visualization, journeying, sounding, breathing, and movement or kinesthetic meditation. I almost always join forms of meditation together when teaching and meditating. Centering and grounding are kinesthetic, visual, and vibrating exercises. The powerful energetic effects of movement, sound, and inner vision produce altered states and increase the flow of the life force through the physical, emotional, mental, and spiritual bodies.

When meditating, I typically do what is possible in the setting in which I find myself. I probably wouldn't do too much sounding in my workplace as I am not really into distracting all my co-workers with my antics or frightening my patients or clients with loud vibrational noises. However, where appropriate, I do what I need to do to enter meditation.

It is enormously helpful to set aside time in the day for the purpose of meditation. Some prefer the early morning prior to the start of the day; for others the afternoon lull is a good time; and for night folk, evening may be best. If you are the busy parent of young children, nap time, sleep time, or anytime possible will do. Whatever the time of day, attempt to meditate regularly at a given time each day. When you become adept at meditation and aware of its results, you may find yourself meditating on a consistent basis throughout the day.

Journey Meditations

Journey meditations are so named because they take us on an inner journey. That journey can be through a forest or beach, out to the sky or universe, into one's self and body, or along a path to other worlds. The mind goes on a journey to discover information or to experience a loving, nurturing, and restorative place. Journey meditations can be used to gather wisdom, retreat from this physical world, meet other souls, or find comfort in solitude. There is no one formula for a journey meditation and no limitation to the purpose of such journeys. The following are simple examples of journey meditations that I have found to assist in healing and opening the soul. These examples are based on the spiritual premises previously discussed in this book. Please remember that the examples I present are uncomplicated frameworks to initiate meditation. There are many other journeys to choose from. The most important aspect of meditation is to do it.

Instructions

For beginners, guided visual journey meditations are often most easily done with an audiocassette that you can listen to with your eyes closed. You can also read a meditative journey first and then do it. Here journey meditations are presented in written form. You may need to read the written meditation several times before doing it.

1. Allow yourself at least fifteen minutes for these meditations. You may find you exceed this time or only manage a fraction of it. Don't worry about how long it takes, just do your meditation, whatever it may be.
2. Before meditating, it is necessary to be grounded, centered, and to clear your mind. Perform the exercises presented previously to achieve an energetically grounded, centered state and a clear mind.

3. Use your imagination to follow the suggested journey.
4. Meditate.
5. When you are ready to end your meditation, gently bring your awareness back to your body, the place where you sit. Slowly open your eyes and breathe and stretch. You may feel very open and need time to adjust to your surroundings.
6. When you have finished meditating, you may wish to record your thoughts, journeys, and other aspects of the experience. This is not necessary, but it may be helpful and enlightening.

Example #1 Journey Meditation
This meditation will be visually guided. Remember, prior to sitting to meditate you must first center or ground your energy. Once you have centered your energy and feel your body's connection to earth, position yourself comfortably with your spine as upright as you are able. Breathe in a relaxed manner. You are now ready to begin the journey meditation.

With eyes closed, focus your attention on the area in your body called the third eye. This is physically located between and above your anatomical eyes and set deep within. As you concentrate on this area, you will begin to perceive a window, a passage, or a ball of light.

Go through this window or enter the light. Follow the light down through your body and into the earth. Feel this light source as it pulsates from the energetic core of the earth up through your body into your pelvis to your central star of light. Feel this light as it radiates out to encompass your entire body and extends out from your center. Move upward through your soul and rest a moment there. Be with your soul awhile. Feel your longing for light and nurturance as you move upward to the gate of entrance to life's source. Go through this gate of light and float up toward the heavens filled with stars. Find your star, the one that beckons to you, and go to it. Alight upon it and let it take you coursing through the night sky, across the universe to a special place. Stay there awhile and journey as you will.

When you are ready to complete your meditation, gently bring your awareness back to your body, the place where you sit, and slowly open your eyes, breathe, and stretch.

Example #2 Journey Meditation

Again, center your energy, position yourself comfortably, and breathe in a relaxed manner.

As you breathe in slowly through your nose and out through your mouth, begin filling your breath with light you draw up from the earth. See the light fill your entire body as it flows up through your legs and into your trunk. Continue to breathe in light and breathe out. With each breath travel upward through your body to your mind's eye. Pass through and enter a magical and wondrous forest. See the magnificent tree that pulls you to it. Embrace the strong trunk of this tree and join with it. Feel its strength, its rootedness, and the natural flow of its energy. Stretch upward with it and move out into the canopy its branches make against the sky. Pause here to wonder. Allow this living tree to speak to you now. Go where you will and absorb the energy offered to you.

Example #3 Journey Meditation

In this journey meditation you are going to meet a wise soul or guardian. You may wish to view this as an extension of yourself or as an extension of God. Whatever understanding makes you most comfortable is fine.

Again, center your energy, position yourself comfortably, and breathe in a relaxed manner. Follow your energy line from the center of the earth. Rise up with it through your body and see the colors that unfold. Traverse with the light as it moves up through your body to your mind's eye. Follow through the window and into a clearing in the woods. A large rock invites you to sit and rest awhile. Hear a running brook and the sounds of the woods as you wait for the guide who is sent to you now. What is it you have need of or desire to know? Allow your guide to teach you and show you what he or she offers you. Stay here awhile and rest in this place.

These three examples are generic meditations whose goal is to start you on your own journey. They are meant to facilitate, not dictate, your journey meditation. I use nature, the skies, stars, and light because they are universal images. When versed in journey meditation, you can create your own personal meditations. There are journey meditations designed to foster physical healing, emotional healing, and spiritual healing.

I have learned much from journeying meditations taught by the Native Americans. All cultures speak of the journey as a path to wisdom and insight. The Jews journeyed through the desert and the early Christians traveled throughout the Middle East. Moses wandered in the desert; Jesus ventured into the wilderness, and the Buddha traveled far before settling beneath the Bo tree. We all journey through life and can journey inward to find ourselves there.

Sounding/Vibration Meditations

Here sounding is used to induce a meditative state. In vibrational sounding, you direct the vibration toward the upper rear palate and ultimately target the third eye. Once you have entered the third eye, you can proceed to higher levels of meditation by continuing to use gentle vibration and allowing your mind to rest in a sea of soothing sound.

To assist in sounding/vibrational meditation, you can play percussion instruments and drum, chant, or simply listen to drumming, chanting, or other music. The process involves first centering yourself and becoming immersed in sound. There are many variations and methods for sounding and vibration. The following examples offer a few ways to induce a meditative state.

Example #1 Sounding Meditation—Humming

Use sound/vibration to center or ground yourself. Close your eyes and begin humming. Consciously send the vibration of your humming through your entire body. Feel the vibration travel down into your feet, your pelvis, your diaphragm, and arms. Hum and vibrate until your entire body feels the vibration and your consciousness begins to lift up with the vibration to focus on the third eye area. Once there, continue to vibrate or hum until you reach an altered state that moves you to a silence in which your whole being is a tingling of vibrations. Sit and be in that still/moving space. When you are ready to end your meditation, bring your awareness back to your body, the place in which you sit or stand, and gently open your eyes.

Example #2 Sounding Meditation—Drumming

Center and ground. Begin drumming a beat at any rate and in any rhythm that feels right. Close your eyes and focus on the sound. Get lost in the sound of each vibration from the drum. Feel the drumbeats move through your body and into the earth. Allow your drumming to change or alter with your senses. Bring the vibration of the drum through your body and to the third eye. Continue drumming as you enter an altered state. When lifted to where you would like to rest, cease drumming and stay awhile there.

When ready to return from meditation, bring yourself back to the room and gently orient yourself to your environment.

Example #3 Sounding Meditation—Chanting

Chanting is similar to humming vibration through the body. There are sacred words used for chanting in many religions and cultures. "Om," "shalom," "amen," "hallelujah," and "ho" are examples. Combining the sounds of vowels and consonants in chanting form produces resonations that move through the body and up into the third eye. Find a series of sounds or words that are meaningful to you or feel good when sounded. For this exercise I will use the chanted phrase "Serenity, serenity, serenity—amen." This phrase should be sounded out emphasizing each syllable of each word: *"sa   ren   eh   tee,   sa   ren   eh   tee,   sa   ren   eh   tee,   ahh   men."* Exaggerate the sounds to vibrate them through your body. The tempo and dynamic level can become quick and loud at first, then slow and low. Center and ground. Close your eyes and begin chanting. Repeatedly chant the phrase, taking breaths when necessary. Build your chanting to a crescendo and level off slowly. Sit in this space and meditate.

When you are ready to end your meditation, bring your awareness back to your body, the place in which you sit or stand, and gently open your eyes.

Kinesthetic/Movement Meditations

Kinesthetic meditations incorporate many forms of movement. You can use anything from tai chi to dance to slight rhythmic motions as you move into and in meditation. I have adapted my exercise regimen to include meditating as I run or cross country ski on my machine. I reach a different level of meditation during rigorous exercise that I use to consciously infuse my physical body with qi or life force. In all meditations I become aware of releasing old or negative energy and breathing in new or positive energy. This breathing occurs through all pores in my body and it is remarkable how light my body can feel when moving and breathing in meditation.

In movement meditation, spiral and diagonal patterns of movement are geometrically and energetically prominent. Neuro-developmentally, spiral and diagonal patterns are the most advanced forms of movement. Babies move at first in simple patterns of bending and straightening, and as they develop neurologically, their patterns of movement become more complex. Gross motor skills advance to include stabilizing the shoulder girdle and pelvis while fine motor skills (grasping and use of hands) develop. Movement patterns begin to include reaching across the body with an arm or leg, turning, and weight bearing on an arm or leg while performing an activity with another appendage. In the first year of life a baby moves from lying to rolling to creeping then crawling and finally walking. The physical body in its neurodevelopmental stages is breathtaking to behold. The reciprocal alternating motion of walking, going up and down steps, and running are precursors to the more intricate and advanced spiral and diagonal movement patterns we see clearly in ballet, baseball, swimming, martial arts, and daily activities adults perform.

Movement is significant to the development of the neurological system. If you desire to advance and maintain your neurological system in adulthood, the practice of kinesthetic meditation is beneficial. We aim for quality of movement in balance and weight shifting, fluidity in spiral and diagonal motions, and strength of musculature for performance and endurance.

If you are out of shape physically you can get in shape very easily with a basic focus on movement. The kinesthetic meditation I present here is relatively easy and uncomplicated.

Kinesthetic/Movement Meditations—Example

For simplicity I will present movement exercises that focus on balance and quality of movement in a meditative state. Those with movement mastery can adapt their own configurations or patterns of movement. Movement meditation, like all forms of meditation, is diverse and unlimited. I suggest doing these exercises barefooted. The meditation can be done with your eyes closed or keep them open to start with until you are comfortable closing them. Music, quiet, or a natural setting can be used here.

Center and ground. Stand with your legs shoulder width apart and your knees slightly bent, arms outstretched softly like wings. Begin to move your feet and toes as if to absorb the energy of the earth. Bring your awareness into your feet as you pull energy up from the earth and into your body. Feel energy as it moves up your legs and into your pelvis and torso. Allow this energy to course up through your midsection and chest and to fill your arms, neck, and head.

Begin to move about slowly and eloquently by shifting your pelvis and raising one leg off the ground. Balance yourself slowly, remaining conscious of the weight-bearing leg filling with energy and the lifted leg poised for further movement. Begin to move your arms in toward your midline with a fluid motion like the petals of a flower closing and then opening up and out. Circle your non-weight-bearing leg out in an arc to the ground and shift your weight to this leg. Raise the opposite leg and repeat the pattern. All the while remain consciously immersed in the movement of energy through your body and delight in the sensation of your body's flowing movements.

Continue moving slowly and gracefully, following your own internal cues. When you feel energized and have reached an altered state, you can continue your movement meditation, basking in your energetic sea, or you can sit to meditate further in this state.

Always bring yourself out of meditation gently.

Group Meditation

Group meditation can be the quickest method for a profound meditative experience because it offers the collective power of numerous souls and bodies joined together for the purpose of touching divinity. Many individuals who have come to my meditation groups or classes state that in solitary meditation they cannot achieve the level of meditation they experience in the group setting. It would be quite difficult for one individual to generate the kind of energy that twelve or more people can.

Group meditation offers mass quantities of life force energy to all present. Energy is shared, it expands and moves. We are part of a community and the community or group experience is an integral part of our soul's development. We can and should embrace the group experience as well as celebrate our individual efforts and experiences in meditation. Both have an important role spiritually. We need to be able to serve ourselves and share ourselves with others.

The ardent spiritual seeker needs to be aware of just what group she is joining. Discriminating between a meditation group and a religious group is important if your desire is to learn meditation and not necessarily to join a cult. I am not saying that if you voluntarily choose to be a part of a personally meaningful religion that you should not. What I am saying is that this book is about meditation, self-examination, and prayer and not about a specific religion. Be aware that too few meditation schools or fellowships exist and that some are really religious sects purporting to teach meditation. The best rule of thumb is to trust yourself. If something doesn't feel right, don't do it.

If you have specific religious beliefs, you can meditate within those beliefs. If you don't have religious beliefs, you can meditate within your spirituality. Meditation in itself is a spiritual discipline, not a religion. It is meant to enhance your own inner growth and your soul's development. In the presence of a group, the power of meditation is enormous. Make sure you feel this is a comfortable group whose views are compatible with your own before you start meditating with it.

When teaching, I provide a written meditation group protocol and purpose to my students prior to the class. It sets forth the intent and scope of the group for people to evaluate for themselves.

I have taught meditation to groups that have included geriatric clients in nursing homes, inpatients in an alcohol and drug rehabilitation hospital unit, health-care personnel, and people from differing backgrounds who have an interest in learning to meditate. It is astonishing to see the difference in the group energy before and after meditation. To illustrate this, I will share with you a meditation experience in a difficult setting.

In a locked alcohol and drug detox unit, life is harsh. Withdrawal is an agonizing process. Men and women may feel that they are literally crawling out of their skins as they attempt to give up heroin, crack cocaine, and alcohol. The inpatients in a detox unit are a mixed group comprising all levels of society. The length of stay for patients varies depending on the specific drugs they are detoxing from as well as their compliance or noncompliance with the course of treatment. They can leave at any time against medical advice, but most had to beg for a spot on the unit. There is a waiting list for most detox units.

As a therapist on such a unit, I led a twice-weekly addiction and recovery group. Quite frequently, angry shouts and slurs accompanied me as I went down the hall to the mandatory group that all patients had to attend with me. The atmosphere was miserable, hostile, and aggressive. These folks were in a great deal of physical, emotional, and spiritual pain. Many couldn't keep from scratching themselves and literally couldn't sit still. They had been through such humiliations as the necessary body search and enema; they were on a locked unit where much of the staff was drained and burnt-out, and they had been thrown into a temporary community of strangers on a ward with no locks on their doors and no real privacy. Needless to say, each group which reluctantly joined me was neither a happy nor a willing bunch.

But that changed with the process of meditation. In the first session, most group participants held hands, learned simple energy grounding techniques, and participated in a journey meditation with me. Afterward, the room would become more still and the group quieted. There were poignant outpourings of feelings and stories of the lives they led which brought them here. There was honesty and hope that maybe they could learn the skills they needed to recover from their addictions. Inner reflection and calm permeated many who before could not sit still.

And though the effect may only have lasted those fifteen to thirty minutes, for some it was to become a pivotal point on their road to recovery.

I could always rely on the fact that the group returning for the final session two days later would greet me with increased fervor and willingness. Of course, I could not count on that the next week when I had to start all over with a new group. Some days require more strength than others.

In a later chapter, I will recount some examples of the power of group meditation, self-examination, and prayer. The joined minds of a group can create miraculous happenings and events. The love that is extended in a group can, indeed, move mountains.

Individual Meditation

Just as group meditation serves our community needs, individual meditation serves our need to know ourselves.

In individual meditation we can begin a course for personal spiritual health and development. The meditations I have shared with you are general energy meditations. Meditations can be adapted to serve therapeutic processes and physical healing. Because a divine force or Higher Power exists there can also be strikingly vivid and recondite spiritual breakthroughs for the individual who meditates. Just showing up and connecting to a higher source through your meditative spiritual disciplines can change the course of your day and life.

There are meditations for forgiveness of self and others, meditations to find the source of illness and discomfort in the body and begin to heal it, meditations for self-acceptance and understanding, and meditations to find your soul's purpose and your relationship to God. Meditation as a spiritual discipline can be used for any personal/group healing needed, and it is a direct way to consciously contact your Higher Power.

Places to Meditate

There are special places on the earth where concentrations of the natural spiritual energy of life force emanate. Often called energy centers, these places facilitate a state of meditation. Perhaps you have visited a location that brought you a sense of peace and increased joy. Such sacred places are often natural wonders or ceremonial/religious locations.

Christianity has sacred places where miracles have occurred; Judaism has the western wall; Native Americans have sacred earth places; and most cultures have holy ground.

A sacred place can be anywhere one chooses to worship God or to join with another in God-awareness. Any place can be made holy by the presence of holiness.

Choosing a place within your home to practice your meditation can enhance your practice. As you become accustomed to meditating there, the space itself becomes the physical location for spiritual practice and assists in centering and grounding. I know when I approach my meditative place I am already sighing a breath of release and solace. It is good to have a sacred retreat within one's home.

Levels of Meditation

Once you become skilled at entering meditative states you can perform many daily activities in a meditative state. The common image of someone meditating in what appears to be a full trance is only one level of meditation. There are other levels of meditation that allow us to interact regularly in the course of a day. Often as I am treating a patient or client I will be in some level of a meditative state. I offer that person my total attention and awareness in addition to communicating a calm, benevolent presence. I find that people respond more openly and feel increased safety when our interaction is perceived as caring and focused on their needs at that time. My meditative state is just that. When I am enriched with meditative energy, I have much to give because my needs have been attended to.

Levels of meditation are not really classifiable. They are subjective for those who meditate. There are those for whom relaxation is meditation. There are many who have spiritual experiences and awakenings in meditation. Each individual who pursues a path of meditation will find within herself ever-expanding levels of meditation.

I would be negligent here if I did not tell you of the gifts of regular divinely-inspired meditation. Often as people become more consciously guided by their intuitions, answers to questions or struggles appear seemingly effortlessly, and they discover a new awareness of people and life in general. Entrance into "other" worlds of spirit and knowledge is possible. Meditation is a strong force and should be regarded as such. Thankfully, Divine Spirit is kind, and you will progress in meditation as you are ready.

Through meditation, I have joined the ranks of people who are able to see, hear, feel, and absorb information that most folks don't appear able to. As a health provider with a degree in the sciences I am grateful that much of this information can be validated by personal interview and medical measure. In a later chapter, I will offer you examples of this ability. Suffice to say I believe all people are equipped with this same ability; they just do not use it. There is an infinite amount of soul power we do not ordinarily use, and meditation is a discipline which, when exercised regularly, brings what could be considered extraordinary gifts. I prefer to call them spiritual gifts because owning them requires a devotion and dedication to cleanliness of living in a spiritual, God-directed way.

The Functions of Meditation

As already mentioned, meditation can heal and help maintain balance and harmony in one's life. Recognized purely as a stress reducer, the effects of meditation on health itself are enormous. A multitude of stress-related illnesses and symptoms can be relieved through effective employment of stress reduction techniques. There has been much written on the apparent relationship between stress and the workings of the immune system in humans. When we are run-down or continually barraged by overwhelming stress without a means to find restoration, we are more likely to become ill or injured. The regular practice of meditation reduces the stress level in our lives by providing the body, mind, and spirit with an opportunity for restoration. In a quiet, stilled framework we can process out the stressors and turn inward for positive, calming energy.

Often, beginners in meditation experience only the calming or quieting peacefulness of meditation. That's quite a feat in our world. Such comfort is exquisite. Circumstances and stressors may not change at all, but our responses to them do because we do not have to be controlled by them. We can pull within, find some inner serenity, and proceed with our day.

Even in illness the ability to meditate is healing. In a peaceful, loving state of meditation the mind, body, and spirit are given an optimum environment in which to flourish. If our inner state is nurtured, we can move toward health on the disease-to-ease continuum. Does this mean that our cancer will be cured, or that our HIV infection will no longer have adverse effects on our physical health? Possibly. Is this a responsible answer to those questions? Yes. Anything is possible, and positive, health-enhancing techniques are a better bet than destructive patterns.

But the more profound answer lies in the mystery of one's individual unfoldment of spirit. I have witnessed "incurable" diseases eventually taking the physical lives of those I loved. Did that signify that they did not achieve health and great measures of soul development? No. For those who grasped their relationship to the divine and used meditation, there were huge benefits, both physical and spiritual. They may have required less medication or used meditation to augment the efficacy of their treatment regimen, stayed healthy longer and gained physical earth time to accomplish a necessary task, and lived each remaining physical moment

more meaningfully than most people do. They, perhaps, connected to their life force line and knew that life continues beyond
the physical world. Perhaps because of their spiritual practices,
they were able to move on to a higher dimension of consciousness
soulfully enriched by their sojourn in physical life. Is this a lesser
miracle than the attainment of a physically healthy body? No answer need be given.

The use of meditation can indeed bring more special results
than just stress reduction. But it also has been demonstrated by
many individuals to bring greater health to the body. The surest
way to find out if this is true is to practice regular daily meditation. Give yourself ninety days. I am quite certain that after ninety
days of regular daily energetic meditation you will be able to decide for yourself if there is benefit to your health. The proof is always in the demonstration. See for yourself if it works.

Meditation is an energetic phenomenon. You will feel a shift
within yourself when you meditate regularly. You will become
more alive and in so doing will experience emotions, situations,
and living, more acutely. This is wonderful and it is painful. When
you have a discipline that teaches balance and movement of energy through your system, things will be moved and felt. It is
therefore essential to include another spiritual discipline in your
daily life. That discipline is self-examination, and it is necessary
for growth.

Chapter 3

✳

SELF-EXAMINATION

To examine the self involves a searching of our own conscience and consciousness. "Examen," the Latin root of "examine," is defined in *Webster's Comprehensive Dictionary* as "a scrutiny or searching of conscience." It is an important aspect of the search for self.

Why would an individual choose to engage in examen? Philosophers have endlessly debated this question through the centuries. My answer draws on the spiritual premise that examen is necessary to fulfill life's purpose, which is to evolve the soul and consciousness. If soul's evolution is the purpose of self-examination, then examen must also involve the dynamic of change. Examen without the ability to change would be fruitless. Therefore, I am proposing that the action of change is inherent to the spiritual process of examen or self-examination. Every spiritual path requires that the participant engage in a soulful examination of the self. One must take stock of one's inner life: the good, the bad, and the unresolved. Spiritually this is necessary so that we can get to our essences, our souls if you will, and find our true selves there. But how, in our modern society, do most of us get there?

The Path to Self-Examination

Many of us do not willingly go through the portal and voluntarily choose daily self-examination as a regular spiritual practice. Sometimes a life crisis is needed to open the doors of self-examination. We may reach a moment in time when we happen to look upon ourselves and see someone we do not know. Perhaps we have become a stranger to ourselves—disillusioned and faltering. Sometimes we are smacked with a dose of reality from a personal tragedy. Illness (either one's own or that of a loved one), divorce, job loss, addiction, depression, and other catastrophic life events can propel us toward the process of self-examination.

Typically, some form of agony brings us to self-question and gives us the courage to look within because the pain is too great not to. This is a time of unsettling uncertainty and taking stock. Who am I? What have I become? Where am I going? Why? Seize this moment. It is a divine gift. Your own soul is calling out to you to bring you home to yourself. It is here in this place of pain where the road does indeed fork. Heed the cry of your heart and take the road less traveled.

The spiritual process of self-examination often begins at this point because few of us have been adequately prepared in this discipline. There is a sweet joke in the twelve-step fellowships: "No one gave me a manual as a child which said this is life and here's how to navigate it." This is funny, sad, and telling of our society.

Communal Wisdom—Lost and Found

We, as people, have made giant strides in technology and science and lost a wealth of wisdom and knowledge in not valuing the communal and/or family elders who were gifted in teaching inner wisdom to the tribe or family. For most of our modern society, those whose function it was to teach insight and awareness of self have been lost for many generations. They have been replaced with a set of values that emphasizes "every man for himself" and "there is not enough for everyone, so get whatever you can."

Our materialistic and superficially skewed view of success and prosperity has kicked aside inner knowing, and our children are taught all the things we value most: money, prestige, physical perfection, and education for those who can afford it. Even our politicians are expected to be corrupt liars who are exempt from the rules the people they represent are supposed to follow. It is no wonder that society is decaying.

Thankfully, there is a movement afoot that is directed at improving our skills at self-examination and inner wisdom. It does not spring from religious extremism or political partisanship. It comes from the emerging number of people who are willing to self-examine to promote change and who value those aspects of our souls that appear to have been forsaken. It is the truth-seeking individual who will once again return to the position of communal wise person and leader. Those with the courage to examine the self are unafraid of group scrutiny. They have already been down that path and know from whence they have come.

Self-Examination As a Shared Experience

So, no one gave us a manual for negotiating life. But there is a process through which we can come to terms with ourselves and our life's purpose. Beginning an extensive inner examination involves a paradox. The most efficient, revealing, and healing self-examination is not done alone. It is done with another. There are several reasons for this. First, for many people, the crisis of selfhood has been established over a considerable time and is rooted in their family backgrounds and environmental influences. Many people would not know where to begin to uncover their own self-truth or how to gain appropriate perspective on their experiences without the guide of a gifted and wise soul.

This is well-illustrated by the twelve-step fellowships' fifth step: "We admitted to God, to ourselves, and to another human being the exact nature of our wrongs." This is not to imply that all we have to share in self-examination are our wrongs, but rather it demonstrates the spiritual healing nature of allowing our innermost secrets and darkness to be exposed to the light and illumination of God and another well-chosen soul. There is a boundless catharsis in the exposure of the self we keep hidden from others and, yes, with or without knowing, attempt to hide from God. The spiritual teaching here is that we have need of one another. When two souls are joined for the purpose of love—and that is what assisting another in finding herself is—God himself is found therein.

Finding a Guide

It is a sacred trust to enter another human being's innermost thoughts and choosing a witness/teacher/guide wisely is of utmost importance. Psychotherapists serve well in this capacity, because they are ethically and legally bound to confidence. Moreover, those psychotherapists who are licensed and regulated have an extensive education in human psychology and have undergone the psychotherapeutic process themselves as a prerequisite to practicing psychotherapy.

Because most of us come to self-examination through some crisis, we may need guidance in finding an appropriate psychotherapist. There are regulatory boards in many states and phone numbers to assist you. In choosing a psychotherapist, a personal interview is essential. Look for someone who is licensed and credentialed. Ask the therapist if he or she has undergone psychotherapy, for how long, and if he or she continues to do so. Do you feel comfortable in the therapist's presence and do you like this person? These are highly important questions, because safety and trust are paramount in a psychotherapeutic relationship.

Why do I feel we need a psychotherapist to sort out the self? Because the right psychotherapist has the proper training to assist an individual in self-examination and, at best, is an exemplary model of self-knowing and contentment. The unhealthy cannot teach health effectively, and so we must choose a psychotherapist on the basis of his or her own apparent psychological health.

You may find a mentor or friend who can serve in this capacity, but often the relationship can become convoluted by other issues that may hamper your self-examination. The clarity of a psychotherapist/client relationship is best, because the focus is on the client. The time spent together is devoted to one purpose—the client's self-examination process. Of course, psychotherapists learn much about themselves in relationship to their clients, but that is not the focus of the relationship. In addition, a psychotherapist will not usually be judgmental, moralistic, or espouse a particular religious point of view. Most psychotherapists strive to be nonjudgmental and to conduct therapy within a humanistic frame of reference. To begin a thorough process of self-examination involves assessing and understanding your personal past and looking to your present self. Unraveling the past requires time and effort. Honesty and thoroughness provide a basis for viewing your life's course and coming to understand the turns you took along life's path.

We must remember at this juncture, that the process of self-examination is a spiritual one, with the goal being to know the self so that we may live fulfilling and passionate lives. This must be kept in mind, because the process of self-examination is often murky and mired in difficult and painful experiences and memories. It can be an uncomfortable process, yet it is the most freeing and life-affirming discipline for the soul. For the sheer beauty and fragility, and the strengths and triumphs, of each individual's exposed inner self exalt the spirit of humanness.

I am passionately in favor of psychotherapy as a method for facilitating the quickest, most detailed, and most ongoingly profound experience of inner searching for the initiate/beginner. The clouds of the past through which we have come are dense, and the layers of defenses and roles we have assumed are vast. To get to our essence with sanity and clarity, we need help. The healthiest, most well-rounded and comfortable people I know have undergone extensive self-examination through the psychotherapeutic process. At its loftiest, psychotherapy offers the modern version of the communal wise person who lives what he teaches and teaches others to teach others the same.

Roadblocks to Self-Examination

It is interesting that in our culture, we judge those who seek psychotherapeutic council as "sick." For in reality, those who do not turn inward to look at themselves are, in effect, running from themselves. They dare not look too deeply, afraid of what they will find. So they repress and deny, remaining unresolved in their inner life. This is not psychological or emotional health; conversely, it is what is "sick."

As a professional occupational therapist, but mostly as a participant, observer, and counselor, I have noticed one area that keeps most people from self-examination: fear. What do we fear? We fear knowing ourselves. As astounding as that may seem, it is the simple truth. We run through our lives in our own particular patterns of madness, whatever they may be—workaholism, obsessive relationships, obsession with material success, addictions, or resignation to a dull, mundane existence—only to come upon the mirror of self, look, and run away. I cannot tell you on how many occasions people will come to me in obvious personal conflict and pain and upon beginning the process of looking within, will abruptly stop once they realize this will require personal confrontation. Most often, they run away as quickly as they can by distracting themselves with other situations or obsessive patterns so as not to have to stay too long with what they see.

What is so frightening within? Is it the possibility that one might have to change? Are the ghosts of the past too painful to feel? Will we have to give up some notion of ourselves that isn't real? I'm certain it is all of these things and many more. The tragedy of it all is that there will be no lasting inner peace until the courage to leap into ourselves is found. Often this courage comes in the form of desperation. For lack of options, the desperate will leap into the unknown and upon taking that leap will find divine grace supporting their flight to the foothold beyond. Once the choice to delve into the self is made, fear may come along, but it no longer immobilizes you.

I have known many people who will consult a therapist or mentor for a specific area of their lives that is painful and will only look as far as they must to patch up that piece which rears its uncomfortable head. They may work on a relationship or an aspect of their personality which gives trouble, but that is where they leave it. To go further would disrupt their lives, and so they never seek further for fear of change. From a spiritual perspective this is a job undone.

The Spiritual Practice of Self-Examination

The spiritual practice of self-examination is thorough and uncompromising. It becomes a way of living that is not evaded. Fear is accepted as a piece of ourselves that has a healthy place in our lives, but fear does not dominate our life's course. I have done many tasks with a certain fear ever-present, and by carrying on despite my fears, I have grown through my fears to greater levels of courage and success. This was not achieved in isolation.

There are those who have been through the process of self-examination and have a spiritual commitment to the process. They are the mentors we seek. Such mentoring is ever-available through gifted psychotherapists, self-help fellowships, or that person down the hall who always seems genuine, connected to life, and real. As a spiritual process it would make sense for self-examination to be a discipline we would need to learn from another. For God speaks through people, and given the opportunity, we can gain the wisdom Divine Spirit gives when we take the extended hand and enter into ourselves with a witness and guide.

Coming to know the self is empowering. When we have searched ourselves and found our souls, we can be free to do our work in this world. We can live out the wonderful dream of our integrated selfhood. Change becomes natural and in line with our heartfelt life's purpose. Had we been taught spiritual self-examination from childhood, probably so much change wouldn't be necessary. But for most of us this is not the case, and now is the perfect time to learn who we are and what we want in life.

Such a realization often comes to those faced with the impending death of the physical life. The extraneous falls away and the real aspects of spiritual living become foremost. If only we didn't need death to awaken us and bring us to truth. And we don't need death. For, from a spiritual viewpoint, life itself is a continuum. We will all surely experience physical death, but the opportunity to find our souls exists throughout this physical lifetime. This life is, in fact, an opportunity to find the soul and move on with an evolved and more complete consciousness. We are here to evolve our souls, and those who do not take the gift to do so only put off the work for another time.

Too few choose the spiritual path, because it does indeed appear the more difficult choice. We must be responsible and accountable. A life lived with self-examination appears arduous. It does not allow for denial, hiding, and masks. It requires integrity, self-love, and earnest searching for self-truth. The difficulty of self-examination, it would seem, is temporal. The lasting oneness with self and freedom wrought from the process are eternal.

Beginning Self-Examination

The process of self-examination can begin at any juncture in the life cycle. Typically, the pressing issue which brought you to "examen" is the place where you begin to uncover the inner self.

We can look at self-examination as two processes. The first is a process that takes place over an extended period of time because it is essentially a life review. Again, this process is done in a psychotherapeutic context with a qualified counselor. The second process is a daily review of events and the self. It is practiced regularly over the course of a day and is designed to keep us attuned to our inner thoughts and the issues current in our lives. These two aspects of self-examination are, of course, not mutually exclusive.

Life Review

We begin with the life-review process of self-examination. This comprehensive approach to self-examination begins in the place where you are. If there is a prominent problem in your life, that is where the process begins. This problem is an opening, a door through which you can enter into yourself and begin to unravel the mysteries that lie within. This process is normally initiated once or twice weekly for an intensive forty-five minute session with a qualified professional psychotherapist.

Here we begin to look at what the issue that led us to seek therapy has done to our lives and just what we can do at this point in time to ameliorate the situation. This complaint could be merely an internal problem or it could be affecting our ability to function completely in the world. The following are some examples of personal crises that bring us to the self-examination process:

1. A state of depression over which we do not feel any control.
2. An addiction that has forced us to finally seek help.
3. A divorce or relationship difficulty that we cannot handle alone.
4. Job loss.
5. Identity crisis.
6. Fear or phobias or anxiety attacks that immobilize us or directly affect our ability to function freely.
7. Death of a loved one.
8. Sickness or illness, our own or that of a loved one.

The above examples need not be what brings us to the life-review process, but overwhelmingly these are the issues that cause people to seek help.

And so we begin at this crisis and start to sort out who we are and how to process the immediate problem so that we can function in the daily course of our lives. This is necessary before we can proceed further and examine the inner realms of self.

Temporarily, these crises can halt our regular lives. When this happens we need immense compassion and assistance. The primary goal of therapy at this time is to get through this critical period to a place of better perspective. If your problem is depression, there may be temporary need of medication. I say "may be" because there are many levels of depression, and some do require medication. If it is an addiction, then the addiction and recovery process must be initiated first. If the crisis is illness, death, or loss, then the accompanying feelings need to be processed and explored. And so on. The means to ameliorate the crisis come first.

But know this: whatever the crisis is, it is temporary and the accompanying pain will subside. Order will be restored to you through the chaos. Those who have gone this way can tell you themselves that although it feels like an abyss of insanity, here is where they began their journey homeward to themselves.

Once the crisis period is brought into some form of balance, the life-review process can begin. Remember that the ultimate goal is to know ourselves and engage in "examen" to discover who we really are.

Life review entails going back to our past and uncovering our developmental experiences as children, adolescents, and adults. This exploration uncovers the dynamics of our primary relationships in our families and the feelings, thoughts, and experiences that were significant in the course of becoming who we are.

This is a consuming and thought-provoking process. It leads us back through our lives to our core experiences and explores the development of our inner life. The life-review process is done in stages over an extended course of time. At times it can appear to "magically" open us to new awareness and seemingly instant insights into our patterns of behavior and inner thoughts and feelings. Some of these shared insights are negative and some are positive. They all bring us closer to knowing ourselves.

If we have been through some trauma, and few among us have not been, we can look at and explore what these experiences did to mold us and examine the defenses we developed to protect ourselves. These defenses may not serve us now. We cannot live in the moment and be free from the shackles of the past if we carry inside ourselves the perspective of a child, reacting to experiences and events which occurred in childhood with a very different set of people and different relationships. And yet, many people continue to live their entire lives from this vantage point and are unable to exist in the present and see that their current relationships are not their childhood relationships and that they are no longer children. They go through life laden with the baggage of the past.

To unconsciously live each new day carrying the weight of unresolved core relationships, conflicted emotional ties to the past, and repressed negative or positive experiences robs us of the unfolding moment and the miracles of a transformed and clear mind. This is a stifled and frozen place that stymies our spiritual development. Fortunately our continued spiritual quest awaits only the decision within each of us to "get our house in order." This can be accomplished through consciously sifting through the unresolved relationships that formed us and the experiences that had great impact upon our lives. Resolution involves coming to an understanding of an experience or relationship so that it no longer blindly drives us, torments us, or undermines our present self. This does not mean that all the pieces of our past will fit together perfectly or that we will have the opportunity to confront or "right" all of our past relationships with the actual players. What it does mean is that we can become whole within ourselves and join the fragmented parts so we may be comfortable with ourselves, stop repeating the past, and move on.

There is a common saying: "We are only as sick as our secrets." This is a very wise, spiritual, psychotherapeutic idea. The attempt of the mind to keep hidden what is viewed as "bad," "terrible," or "sinful" creates more mind sickness. Our secrets fester and rot within and fear that the truth of our dark selves may become known takes over. But in a relationship to a Higher Power, there are no secrets. All is revealed and all is known. The revelation of our secrets to a wise trusted sage and in the presence of Divine Spirit breathes light and freedom into the mind and soul. Our secrets reveal our humanness and their revelation brings the healing process to our inner life. We no longer need to live in fear of our secrets being found out. When we look within ourselves with the hand of another and God, we find catharsis and relief in the courage of self-revelation.

The course of self-examination and life review leads us through windows of self-knowledge. We come to see ourselves: our essence and humanness, who we have been, and who we are. And it is here that we can decide, with a clear mind, who we want to be and what our passion and purpose in life are. For clear inner vision, unburdened by the chains of unknowing, can allow for the present self to grow and move in a chosen direction. We can cultivate those relationships and experiences that feed and nourish our cleansed souls. We can decide what to cut away and what to keep, what is valuable and what is valueless in the scheme of our lives. We can be in a place that is present to live each day, for the insurmountable past has become the sand beneath our feet upon which we walk. Self-examination is an ongoing spiritual process as is the life journey. Once we have initiated and conducted an extensive life review, we can assimilate and integrate our life's experiences and have a conscious and pulsating awareness of our inner self.

There are a multitude of personality types and patterns of relating to the world. Each self-examination pilgrimage is unique to the individual who undergoes the process. What needs to be forgiven? What fears need to be acknowledged? What wonderful sweetness resides within? How do we change our old dysfunctional behavior and adapt to the self we have found and desire to nurture? These are some of the questions to which the process leads us.

Actually living life through this spiritual process is a test of our being. As with any new task, piloting our newfound consciousness relies on a system of trial and error. The people, places, and circumstances around us may not change, but we have changed. Self-knowledge is empowering. It affords us the ability to make conscious, well-thought-out choices that we can accept responsibility for and follow through on. It promotes integrity, self-honesty, and self-trust. And although those around us may resist our empowered, conscious self, we make a way to manifest our truer self and identity in the world.

We may have family members, friends, or lovers who are unable to accept our changing or self-discovery. This can be worked out in time, although there is most probably emotional pain inherent to the process. For, in time, gaps can be bridged or the limitations of certain relationships can be temporarily accepted. I say "temporarily" here only because all people have the potential for growth, and therefore all relationships have the same potential.

Individuals who have undergone the psychotherapeutic, spiritual life review will emerge more in touch with their emotions and thoughts and more able to actively connect their inner life to their outer life.

This means several things. You will more acutely and consciously experience all things, and you will learn to integrate, assimilate, and process these experiences at ever-deepening levels of awareness. This is good news when you consider positive emotions such as joy, love, and harmony. But even through life's difficulties and sorrows there is joy in fully experiencing the depth of personal pain. For when you allow yourself to fully grieve, mourn, or hurt, you can move on unfettered by residual or repressed suffering. And you find new ways to accept and use what are considered negative emotions to improve your well-being.

Anger is often considered a negative emotion. It is such a powerful force, full of explosive energy. Anger can be channeled to create masterpieces and charge your battery for new challenges and tasks. Instead of repressing anger and not allowing it to swell and rise within, take it and ride it in a healthy and focused manner. Go for a run or walk steadfastly up a mountain; clean out that closet that's been collecting garbage for years. Let your energy be used for purposeful, and not destructive, activity, and in releasing this force you will again find balance.

There are those who believe that a spiritual life is devoid of anger, depression, fears, or deep passion of any kind. They expect one who claims to live spiritually to fit an ideal image of an imagined perfect being. To this I say, where are the steps in between? The links that join humanness to Divine Spirit? These links are seen in those who attempt to bridge the earthly and the celestial. Such individuals accept the task of their humanness and bring divine aspects of their spirituality into their lives on a regular basis. These individuals are willing to go through the rigors of life in a real manner that does not deny human weaknesses and faults but seeks to transcend them. This is only done through trial and error, success and failure. We are not perfect or we would not be here, but we have the possibility, with each new moment, of coming closer to that way of living which brings us inner comfort and peace. The life-review process offers an opportunity to seize this possibility: it reveals us to ourselves and brings us to a beginning. From this moment we can proceed in any direction we choose.

The psychotherapeutic life-review process offers us a foundation for evolving our spiritual life. Through this process we come to know a few key factors about our life journey:

- Where we have been in our lives.
- Who we have become in our lives.
- What our strengths and weaknesses are.
- What is important to us.
- Which patterns of living may or may not serve us.
- Who we are beneath it all.
- What we would like to cultivate, and what needs to be excavated.

If we truly experience the spiritual, psychotherapeutic life review we are freed to move into the current day with an internal agenda that is focused on the present moment. We no longer unwittingly carry into every new moment an unhealing self that is bound to the past.

For those who would like to read more about psychotherapeutic life review, there are numerous good books dealing with dysfunctional families, different personality types, the death and dying process, grieving and illness, addiction and recovery, and relationship patterns. This book is not intended to explore the psychological dynamics or mechanisms of all of these processes. This chapter on self-examination illuminates the spiritual task of these processes, brings us to know our inner self, and prepares us to live life in a fully aware and inner-connected way.

Daily Self-Review

Daily self-review is a continual assessment of ourselves and our experiences throughout the day. It fosters a means for staying in touch with the inner self and acknowledges the inner life as important to us. It keeps us in touch with our thoughts, feelings, and experiences and provides us with a time to consider changing that which we wish to change, to appreciate that which we feel good about, and to reflect on that which we shall just "be" with. Daily review is grist for the mill of our minds. As a spiritual process it keeps us listening to our inner voice or soul. It does not allow an excess of clutter to develop. Setting aside specific periods in the day for self-review is an excellent practice for the spiritual initiate. This time can be used to simply review the day's events and our relationship to them, and to listen to our thoughts and feelings, which can offer us plans of action. Self-review can be done prior to meditation or prayer. It is a spiritual discipline that assists us in evolving our soul, because we take time to listen to our soul. Once you become proficient at inner listening and self-review, you'll find yourself naturally employing these processes throughout the day. When we practice disciplines regularly and the benefits of clarity, inner knowing, and open-mindedness are laid bare, we discover a limitless world of opportunity for growth and joy.

Daily self-reviews become a means for us to challenge ourselves to deepen the connection to a Higher Power and the Divine that exists within us. Daily review helps us develop the character traits that spiritual people seek: honesty, integrity, openness to change, responsibility, and a sense of humor. Yes, a sense of humor. It is absolutely delightful to laugh at ourselves in the spirit of genuine love. Laughing at the absurdity of our foibles and ridiculous thinking is an indication of good inner health. There are times when I become divinely aware of my own particular spiral into an old pattern of behavior or thinking and watch myself in review like a cartoon character in a short. It is certainly a divine blessing to have a hearty laugh at myself and move on.

Daily review keeps us current with ourselves, which provides a foundation for changes in behavior, changes in thinking, and changes in relating to ourselves and the world. If we have been short-tempered or impatient or angry, we can observe and listen, understand, and seek to change. If we have been of service to ourselves or others, extended love in a difficult situation, been true to ourselves and handled a trying time well, we can appreciate and enjoy the fruits of our practices and learn to love who we are, warts and all. Our virtues are the results of a life whose devotion is to the spiritual path of evolving the soul toward greater good within. Our inner work surely manifests itself in the outer world and many can attest to the real changes wrought in their lives through a path of self-examination.

It is important to note here a criticism that is often aimed at the process of self-examination. It comes from a belief system that sees involvement with the inner self and acknowledging one's own feelings as "selfish." Most often this critique comes from those whose relationship with the self-examiner is disrupted by the process. The misperception of "selfishness," it would seem, stems from those who do not self-examine and do not want others to change, set limits or boundaries on their relationships, or take control of their own lives. Thankfully, Divine Spirit embraces the self-examiner and ultimately the gifts of inner connection and self-responsibility are bestowed on those on the spiritual path.

The self-examiner is indeed "selfish"—in a wonderful way. This paradoxical "selfishness" imbues the self-examiner with many selfless and generous qualities in community with others. For one who examines the self learns to communicate and listen astutely. Skills acquired through spiritual self-examination include compassion, sharing of thoughts, feelings, and experiences, and caring for oneself. The self-examiner naturally becomes better able to be present with others in an eloquent and meaningful way. Those who are aware of their own needs and feelings are able to be better attuned to the inner voices and real needs of others. For when the self is well-tended and cared for, there is an abundant amount of self to share with others. Self-examining individuals strive toward virtuous and thoughtful behavior and deeds.

It is worthwhile to observe here that the world in which we live is not filled with self-examining paragons of virtue. The self-examiner sees this, and quickly learns that although one can be compassionate, loving, and caring, one also needs the strength of setting limits and boundaries. These limits protect and serve both the inner self and the integrity of the individual in a community.

The good need the strength and power which come through a healthy road of self-examination. When you are centered and focused, you are very strong. I use the word "good" above to describe self-examiners, because the spiritual goal of self-examination is to evolve the soul. I have a spiritual teacher who has often said, "Only the good, self-question." So no matter where you have been or what darkness you have seen, when you begin to self-question, you are on a road toward goodness.

Daily review can be used to facilitate an ongoing psychotherapeutic or mentorship process. Inner reflection and leaps in awareness usually occur between scheduled therapy or supervision sessions. I have found a need to continue to have someone I trust know my thoughts, feelings, and experiences on a "week-in-review" basis. It keeps me honest and ever-growing.

Self-Examination with a Group

Fellowships, support groups, and friends gathering to share self-reflection and experiences are powerful for individual growth. When individuals join together to promote healing and fellowship by sharing the joys and sorrows of life, the force of truth, compassion, and nonjudgment is startling to the newcomer or observer. How could so many lay bare their innermost thoughts to a group of strangers? The effect of self-revelation and earnest communication with others is transforming. As any of us who have been to a fellowship devoted to honest self-examination and spiritual living can attest, the spirit of divine grace descends upon the room and a supernal love envelopes all those present. For in the integrity and joined willingness of those souls gathered, the grace of God exists. And though many cannot precisely name it, they say the same thing over and over again: "I felt like I came home after I came into these rooms." We are coming home when we commit to self-examination and sharing our journeys to find our soul's truth.

The spiritual discipline of self-examination is, in essence, a coming to know the self. It is not an easy process and does not ensure freedom from the pain of living. There will be tragedies, depressions, and unavoidable minor and major crises in life. The beauty and majesty of the self-examination process are in the ability to be fully present and experience these problems with a willingness to be true to the self and learn through them. When we approach these experiences with integrity and courage, they stretch our growth potential (even when we don't want to grow) and engender authenticity and an ever-deepening connection to our Higher Power.

The unseen hand of the Higher Power is ever-available to us. In fact, the most powerful guidance received through self-examination comes from the knowledge that we do not go alone to this place but are lovingly held in the palm of God's hand. This knowledge leads us to the next spiritual discipline explored in this book: prayer.

Chapter 4
✳

PRAYER

Prayer is the most powerful of the spiritual disciplines. There are many reasons for this but the primary reason is that in the act of prayer, we acknowledge our relationship to the Divine, the Creator, or God. We are praying to something: a power or force greater than ourselves. In that simple acknowledgment lies the medium of miracles, the glory of surrender to a will greater than our own and the infinite joy and peace that await us.

Prayer, perhaps more than any other spiritual practice, will reflect back to the one who prays with her perception of who God is. At first, we all come to prayer with our preconceived or childhood notions of God. These are often molded by our religious upbringing or lack thereof. We can observe our approach to prayer to help understand these notions and to move beyond them. How do we pray? From what posture or inner feeling do we pray? From what life circumstances do we pray? When do we pray? These are all significant questions. They can guide us in understanding the restrictions in our relationship to spirit and also our growth in spiritual maturity and spiritual power as our relationship to the Divine evolves.

At this juncture, I must explain my concept of who or what the Creator is so that the reader may know what I am speaking about when I speak of God. Of course any attempt to define the Creator is to limit him, and God is infinite. I, on the other hand, am a human being working within the bounds of my earthly experience using language to express the inexpressible. Everything that I say to describe God has been said in some form before. Great men and women have walked the earth and told us of God. However, I feel that without an explanation of my concept of God this entire chapter on prayer would be meaningless.

God is love. God is unspeakable inner joy and bliss. To be with God is to be without needs, for all is fullness and perfect union. God is the Father, the Mother, the One. When one is with God, there is nowhere else to go, for one is home. One rests in an infinite cascade of peace and light. God is breath and stillness. All yearning comes from our desire to join with God, to be full, at peace, joyous, and home. May you know the Divine Creator in your hearts. Ho.*

The Power of Prayer

The purpose of this book is to demonstrate the healing and the power that a life devoted to spiritual practices brings to the practitioner. The good news is that we can see the workings of the Divine in human life experiences and the power that prayer brings when practiced as a spiritual discipline. No matter what your present relationship to God is, you can learn to bring prayer into your daily life to heal yourself, find your life's purpose, and live life more fully. Knowing your current perception of the Divine will assist you in your spiritual development and ability to pray with increasing power.

What do I mean when I say pray with power? Isn't all prayer powerful? Isn't all prayer heard?

Let me answer the second and third questions first. Yes, all prayer is powerful and, yes, all prayers are heard. To pray with increasing power means to pray from an inner place of clarity with relationship to Spirit and to pray with a faith and wisdom that spring forth from that inner place.

Let me give you an example. In a serious crisis, can you think of one or two people whom you would especially like to be praying for you? Why? Do they possess some special magic or key to the Divine that others you know do not? I know several people I would ask to pray for me if I needed prayers because I know that

---

*Ho is an affirmation/exclamation said at the end or the beginning of a prayer in Native American tradition as amen is said in the Judeo-Christian tradition.

they are closely joined to Spirit and very powerful in prayer. This is not because they possess a gift that all cannot share in, for all can. It is because they have developed that gift that they have the ability to communicate with the Divine deeply, consistently, and ardently. When in prayer, they are clear channels, mostly devoid of ego, and pleasingly united to the larger realm of Spirit.

These people have practiced the art of prayer regularly and their ordinary life is "prayerful," though not necessarily religious. I must make the distinction here, for although some of the people I am speaking of may practice a certain religion, when they are in prayer they have a universal connection to God. I would not ask them to pray for me because they practice a certain religion or have a specific religious affiliation. I would ask them to pray for me because I know their praying is an earnest and larger-than-religion communication to God. This is important, for although we may belong to a specific religion, the prayer I speak of in this chapter is a personal and direct universal line to the Infinite.

The power of prayer comes from the clarity of our relationship to self and to the Divine. The development of one's spiritual relationship to self and the Divine is a process. Some of us appear born with a certain knowledge of the existence of a Higher Power and some of us have come to it through living, and some still reject it outright. That is their option: their free will was granted by the Creator. To be a true student of spirit is to be tolerant and compassionate in our opinion of others' beliefs. I have known atheists who lived very good, beneficent lives, and I have observed the so-called religious condemn all but those who share their rigid belief system.

Two points have been established thus far. To become prolific and powerful in prayer, you must clearly know your perception of the Divine and you must practice prayer.

Most of us are familiar with foxhole praying, that is, praying only when we are in deep trouble. We may also know the rote prayers we recited from youth: prayers of asking, prayers for forgiveness, and prayers of affirmation. The mystically high form of prayer, knowing and joining with the One Mind, is seldom achieved by those who do not learn the way of prayer. In this form of prayer there is no asking and nothing to affirm. All Is.

There is nothing for you to do except become one with the Divine Force that is. This is an ecstatic experience wherein transformation and progression for the physical, emotional, and spiritual self occur. This is the soul's home.

What Is Your Relationship to God?

There are endless ways to incorporate prayer into your daily life. The key is to establish a personal relationship with your Higher Power that is indefinably your own intimate communication and rings true to the core of your being.

What is your relationship to God? Is it an authoritarian parent-child relationship, a nonpersonal one, an angry one, a nonexistent one? Perhaps it is a certain and good one, and you just desire to evolve more spiritually.

The key to the power of your praying (not the power of God) is your relationship to Divine Spirit. To come to know Divine Spirit, you can practice the spiritual discipline of prayer. Sorting out your relationship to Divine Spirit and your perception of the Higher Power involves an intimate and personal journey.

There are some fundamental aspects of Divine Wisdom that if accepted with an open mind can assist you in developing a deep and powerful relationship to Spirit through prayer:

FIRST, God already knows you. You are embraced and enfolded in the Higher Power's love even if you do not know it. There is no secret, no part of you, that is not revealed to God.

SECOND, we humans are imperfect and are searching for wholeness of body, mind, and spirit. In fact, it is the task of our physical sojourn to evolve in body, mind, and spirit.

THIRD, all the spiritual tools we need are at our beck and call, if we would only endeavor to use them.

When learning how to pray, we are really learning how to join with God and allow God into our lives on a conscious, regular basis. If we would accept the reality that we are inherently united with a magnanimous, infinitely loving and wise being commonly referred to as God, much of what troubles us would fade. The simple purity of faith is what moves mountains. The faith we seek is the faith of the child. It is an instinctive reliance on one who knows and can do all. Look to any great mystic, sage, or spiritual leader and you will see there is or was plainly an unshakable belief in and reliance on God. Such faith is very pure, very artless, and all-powerful.

Longing

We all have desires, goals, and dreams. They are not apart from God. Our truest aspirations and long-held dreams are our spiritual proddings and motivators. There is nothing more joyous to the Higher Power than one of his children finding and following her deepest and dearest longing. Longing belongs to the soul and is the soul's way of speaking to you.

Prayer brings unfoldment of your dreams. Prayer guides you on the path of following your longing. It brings direction, comfort, and peace.

The Concept of Will

Self-will gets a bad rap in spiritual circles because it is seen as embodying all aspects apart from divinity. Lust, greed, evil, and moral decay are all associated with the term "self-will." But we truly need to make a distinction between positive and negative self-will. Positive self-will has an affinity for Divine Spirit and gives us a force with which to live and create. It is not "bad" at all. In fact, it was given to us by the Creator himself and differentiates us from all other living things. We were given free will and it is up to us to use our will to advance or retreat spiritually.

The concept of surrendering to the will of God must be addressed here, as many in spiritual fellowships will readily tell you that until they were able to surrender their self-defeating and imprisoning self-will they were unable to walk upon the road of personal healing. This does not mean that the only will they possessed was a self-destructive one. It does mean that up until their surrender they were largely driven by negative self-will. Until they were willing to surrender the only will they were consciously aware of (the negative will) and become teachable, they were unable to learn of the positive will that is a part of them as well and is linked to our Higher Power. Therefore, self-will can either join us with the greater will of our Higher Power or separate us from our own divinity.

In prayer, of course, we are seeking union with our Divine Self, and will plays a monumental part in our finding this self. We possess the will to struggle forward, even amidst despair. We possess the will to overcome adversity, pain, and suffering to find peace. We possess the inner will to achieve beyond our highest aspirations. Yes, indeed, will is a great force in our lives, be it positive or negative.

In prayer, knowing one's own will and attempting to align with the Divine Will takes an extraordinary and delicate balance that even the greatest spiritual minds have wrestled to achieve. A spiritual tool to assist us in this difficult enterprise is the knowledge that the Divine Will is compassionate and beneficent to all even when we lack understanding of it. All prayer is entered into with the affirmation that the Divine Will prevails. This sounds easy. It is inordinately difficult when we have an investment in the outcome of our prayer requests. Our Higher Power knows of our personal investments. We can acknowledge our earnest wishes and yet practice our prayer with the faith that "Thy will be done."

How can this be? Another spiritual truth reveals that suffering is of man, not of God. Our Higher Power's wish for us is to find peace. In the course of our human lives we are bound to come up against situations which produce feelings of suffering. But what is it that suffers? Is it our bodies, our minds, our souls? If we truly understood our own eternal beingness and the love that surrounds and envelopes us infinitely, we would not suffer so. Our own ideas regarding life and the lessons each soul must learn can indeed wreak havoc in our lives. We take a giant leap in spiritual growth in each moment that we realize that God's love for us does not include our need to suffer. We are tortured by our own lack of understanding. Are we tortured by loss of the physical body? It was temporary anyway. Are we tortured by loss of a loved one? Our loved one is with us still, only we in physical body appear unable to continue the relationship, for it is different now. Do we suffer over injustices? These are the injustices of people, not of the Higher Power. We were given free will and there are those who do not use it to promote love and fellowship.

What has all this to do with prayer? Everything. Divine Will for us is always magnificent and celebratory. It is only we, as limited humans, who undergo drastic levels of pain. And this is exactly what prayer is for: to lessen our pain, to bring us joy, to allow Grace to enter humanity. Prayer is a divine gift of communication to God. It is the medium of miracles. The most powerful people of prayer know that God's will for us is always untold love, even amidst apparent human suffering, and because of this, they are able to be channels for this love on earth. And you can be, too, as you learn to practice these principles in your life.

The task of the spiritual student is a challenging one. For how, even in a circumstance of personal devastation, does one maintain faith in the supreme love of the Divine? By willingness. By trying. If you attempt to pray daily and embrace the metaphysical concept that the Higher Power's will for you is to achieve inner peace and serenity, you will achieve it. Even if the moment or instant of inner peace is fleeting, once you have experienced this peace, you will make your way back to it with increased ease.

If you practice prayer as a dialogue of open willingness to explore, listen, and share with the Divine on a regular basis, when you hit the bumps in life's road you will be amply prepared and can draw upon spiritual guidance to undertake the opportunities presented to you.

Spiritual Building Blocks

I use the term "spiritual building blocks" to define those aspects of spiritual character that are developed with prayer and are

sources of power in a spiritual life. None of these spiritual building blocks is new—there is nothing new under the sun.

WILLINGNESS   Willingness precedes all other spiritual
building blocks. It is the master key in spiritual development.
If we lack faith, but are willing to try for it, faith will come. If
we lack understanding or are full of fear, but are willing to
forge ahead and search for it, understanding will come.
Willingness represents our spiritual surrender to a Power
greater than ourselves. When willing, we admit, "I do not
know the way, but I am willing to learn." The Divine Spirit
embraces willingness. Willingness demonstrates an open
mind, humility, and the acknowledgment of a Force greater
than ourselves.

FAITH   Some people are born with faith; others have to
learn it. Here of course, we are speaking of a faith in our
Higher Power's divine will for us. Faith is the knowledge that
the Almighty's will for us is always truth, peace, and comfort.
Faith is knowing that we are never alone, that the hand of
God is always upon us. Faith can be learned through willingness.

TRUST   Trust and faith are quite inseparable. Each is learn-
able. When we allow ourselves to trust in our Higher Power
and in divine wisdom even tentatively at first, the result of that
trust will speak for itself. As we realize the benefit of sacred
trust in our lives, trust becomes the natural order of being.

HONESTY   There is nothing but honesty in relationship to
God. To attempt to hide anything from the divine is to be like
a child who upon hiding his own eyes thinks he cannot be
seen by others. Divine Spirit already knows us and is immensely compassionate in understanding that we may need
to remove our hands from our eyes one finger at a time.

PATIENCE   Patience is my least favorite of the spiritual
building blocks, therefore Spirit generously offers me a continuous supply of opportunities to develop it. Patience
springs forth from trust and faith, and allows us to remain

quiet since we know all will be well. My version, unfortunately, is "I have faith and trust so let me know right now!" As I have said, Spirit is kind to me and allows me to grow enormously in this area.

TOLERANCE   We learn tolerance as we learn the way of Spirit. Divine love is infinitely tolerant of us all as we grow through life. Spiritual students learn to be tolerant of their own apparent limitations and those of others around them. This does not mean we allow unspeakable deeds to be perpetrated around us in tolerance. We do not. No one should tolerate the violation of another human being's rights. The tolerance we speak of here is allowing differences of opinion, beliefs, and cultural ways. No one should force her belief system upon another, for that is not the way of divine wisdom. Spirit is always certain in itself and kind to each soul. That is the way we should be in our tolerance of ourselves and others.

There are many other attributes of the spirit that come with spiritual practice. Courage, generosity, humility, humor (hopefully), and persistence are some of them. These are a natural extension of the spiritual building blocks defined above. But I have chosen willingness, faith, trust, honesty, patience, and tolerance for definition because they are prominent in developing the self in prayer. When we pray with a sense of all of these characteristics, we are praying with power.

Our Prayerful Voice

If we approach our Higher Power with the understanding that it is we who need to open up and communicate, we are establishing the true relationship of the created to the Creator. The Almighty does not expect us to come to prayer as perfected spiritual beings. The Divine Spirit already knows our nature. We must come to prayer as we are, flaws and all, and pray from that stance. This is where healing the self begins.

We can begin our prayer, our communication to God, from this willing, honest place:

"Hi God. It's me. I have been very confused these past two days, and I'm not feeling very good about myself. My life is so crazy. There's so much pressure and I've been yelling at the kids and angry a lot. I feel so down. Could you help? I know I ask that a lot, but I really don't know where else to turn. Thanks for listening, God. I love you."

"Dearest Father,
I am filled with gratitude today. I feel as if I am making great strides in all areas of my life. I feel very close to you and that comforts me. Thank you for being with me. I love you."

"God,
I just don't know where you are. I cannot feel you, touch you or get close. Where are you? I'm sick, I'm angry and I'm all the things I'm not supposed to be. I know you're there, but I'm very far away right now. Please help."

These three communications are simply conversations between a human personality and God. But each communication establishes powerful spiritual building blocks: a willingness to be open to a Higher Power and some personal honesty.

For beginners in prayer, learning how to speak to God with your own personal voice is the start of something big! When you approach God in this way, you begin the process of the Divine Spirit being revealed to you. An invitation is issued by the one who prays, and the Divine Spirit always responds to an invitation. Thus, the cosmic journey of your life can begin.

The three short prayer examples above typify two types of prayer: an "asking" prayer and an "affirmation" prayer. They are by no means the most eloquent or what spiritual authorities might consider the highest forms of prayer (let us laugh here) but they contain the essential ingredient for prayer development: your own voice, your own self coming to Spirit. "Dear Almighty One, I would like to come to know you and myself."

As you develop a personal style of prayer, you will also find ways to increase your proficiency at seeing the results of prayer in your life. Pray often. Pray daily. Pray at the beginning and closing of the day. A moment of prayer is a powerful moment. Your prayer need not be elaborate. A check-in with the Spirit is okay. It's a way to begin. Asking Divine Spirit to assist you in your daily schedule and remembering and acknowledging your connection to a Higher Power as often as you are able affirms that you are not here alone. The results will be remarkable. As with the other spiritual disciplines, you will get tangible personal results from prayer.

The Request and Response

Upon a request to enter your life, the Divine Spirit will respond. Then, as they say in twelve-step circles, "Strap yourself in, you're in for the ride of your life!" Everything about you that requires change will pop up and greet you. The fantastic thing is you won't have to do it alone. Once you call upon your Higher Power, you will feel that presence in your life guiding you.

For beginners prayer can work like this: Take a circumstance in your life that you feel no control over. It can be anything from a problem at work to a relationship difficulty or a health complaint. Tell yourself you are choosing to give this problem to the Higher Power in the form of a prayer each time it comes up in your thoughts or each day until an answer or response to the problem emerges. Take the problem to the Divine Spirit and talk about it. Tell all. Then say, "I can't deal with this by myself and I'm giving it to you, Dearest Spirit." Then affirm that the Higher Power will help (even if you're not sure of this), and get on with your day. Remain open to possible nudges and responses from Spirit.

Each time the problem presents itself to you, give it to God. This does not mean you are not doing anything about the difficulty; it means you are giving it to Spirit to help you sort it out. Do not impose a rigid time frame for an answer. Some answers appear lightning fast and others take time in the working. Wait and look for the guidance given. Spiritual guidance can come in any form, for Divine Spirit can use all form for its purpose. The answer may be spoken through another human being or the right book may appear before your eyes. The answer may come to you upon awakening from sleep or it may slowly grow over the course of the week. Be open, willing, and give it to Spirit. You will receive a response.

Prayer is spoken in thoughts. You may speak your thoughts out loud, but prayer originates in your own mind.

Thinking or thoughts directed to a Higher Power are prayers. Because this is so, prayer is very easy to do. You can have conversations with God anytime: driving to work, at your job, in your bed at night, whenever. Just switching your thoughts to the Higher Power and the Divine Spirit is praying.

Once you begin to establish an opening within yourself to a Higher Power, things are going to happen. To put it plainly, if you have a boil, it may finally require lancing; if you are in a bad relationship, you may finally decide to do something about it, and so on. The flip side of these uncomfortable experiences is that wonderful and fulfilling experiences will present themselves. There will be a clearing out of the negative or unnecessary and an abundance of positive and affirming experiences will become available.

Unfortunately, most of us do undergo some discomfort when we invite the Divine Spirit into our lives if we have been living a life that was not totally aligned with our own personal divine truth. Remember, most of us were making life decisions while we did not know we had more self-harmonious and healthier options available to us. So the crux of the matter is that when you invite divine wisdom into your life, not everything you are going to find out may be comfortable. This is temporary. As you weed the garden of your life with the assistance of Spirit, eventually the weeds are fewer and farther between and not so overwhelming. The weeds serve a purpose as well. They have brought us to see ourselves.

The request to a Higher Power will bring dramatic changes in your life. Learning to lean on divine wisdom first and in all circumstances becomes a habit through prayer. Upon waking you can offer the day's events to God, and throughout the day you can acknowledge divine assistance. It will never fail. Try it. In any situation, ask for Spirit's help and see what unfolds. Try not to preconceive an outcome to a specific situation, and stay open to the possibilities that may be offered by Spirit. You will be amazed that the situation may turn out in a way or manner you never even considered.

As you see the magnificent workings of prayer and divine guidance in your life, you may wonder, "Hey, why didn't I do this all along?" The results of reliance on a Higher Power are indisputable. The best possible outcome for you is always provided. Of course you may not be aware of this fact at that moment, but it will be shown to be true in retrospect.

All you need is willingness to embrace prayer. Do this and faith and trust will become natural extensions of the results provided to you by the Divine Spirit. The Higher Power does not fail when called upon, and through the Higher Power you will learn faith and trust if you lack them.

Thus far we have been speaking about learning how to pray, how to develop your own voice and personal connection to a Higher Power, and how to see the results of a Higher Power's response in your life. An intimate and heartfelt connection to a Higher Power is the foundation upon which all so-called "healing" rests. I have kept the dialogue between self and God simple for a reason. It is in simplicity that we come to know God. Approach the Divine Spirit as a child would approach a loving, nurturing being, and you are there.

Because healing the self requires a holistic and comprehensive approach, three spiritual disciplines have been introduced: meditation, self-examination, and prayer. The following chapters will explore the way linking these three inseparable disciplines leads to the power to heal the self.

Chapter 5

✳

JOINING THE
ENERGY
PRACTICES

Meditation, self-examination, and prayer as actively practiced spiritual energy disciplines serve to evolve our souls. Our souls hold the essence of who we are and what our deepest longings and spiritual goals are in this world. Our souls are also directly connected to Divine Source and, as such, hold the wisdom of divinity and the power to realize our truest, soul-felt dreams in this physical lifetime. To reach our souls and listen to them, we use the spiritual disciplines. The three simple energy practices can unlock the doors to our own brilliant, joyous, and life-filled souls.

Our inner life is an ongoing journey and is as dynamic and ever-shifting as the world in which we live. We have relationships that help us learn and grow, work in the world that challenges our skills and intellect, and new lessons that replace others already learned. We are ever growing and evolving. The soul's evolution is a dynamic process and our spiritual disciplines aid us in that process by moving continually with us and processing our experiences, informing and enlightening us as they join us to Divine Spirit. They are the perfect practices to find, listen to, and continue in order to evolve our souls in consciousness. Through these practices we lift the veil of unknowing to reveal our own soul's truth and journey to our awakened consciousness.

Beings of Energy

We are beings of energy. We have a consciousness and a soul created by God. Put that divine consciousness, soul, and energy into a flesh and blood human body and you have a conscious, divine human being. The only difficulty that arises once the soul enters the human body and takes its own human breath is that most often it enters into a world of humans who have forgotten their own divine energy and think they are only human bodies with the physical limitations of flesh. This perception is backward. We are energy beings in an energetic system that actually creates the human body. Each human body has an energy system that comprises the life force line that holds both the chakra system and soul system within it. The human body is a temporary energy system for the soul. The human life cycle offers opportunity for learning and soul growth. The physical body is a place where time appears to have meaning and events appear to happen in a sequence so that we, as souls, can learn. It is kind of like a classroom for slow learners. Enjoy the laugh.

If you begin to view yourself as an eternal being of energy you can easily understand the energy concept of the human body. Energy is vibration, light, color, and sound. It has a frequency. The body is simply energetically denser than the soul and spirit. Without the soul and spirit, the body is energyless. It dies and decays. Without the soul, the body has no conscious awareness, no eternal reality. It is simply a neutral vessel. The human body is anatomically and structurally able to hold the soul, mind, and spirit and have its cells and form infused with eternal life force. Although most people can't see these anatomical and physiological energy systems yet, they are there. These systems are known as the chakra system and the life force soul system.

Imagine how people thought about themselves prior to the discovery of the human circulatory and nervous systems. They probably knew they bled when they were cut or had pain when injured, but they did not have visual awareness of their entire circulatory and nervous systems. They did not possess the biological and physiological knowledge with which most nonmedical people today are familiar. Progressing further in history, even when the first diagrams of human anatomy were established, the inner workings of the systems were largely unknown. It took many years for science to advance in its understanding of the nervous system and to establish that the nervous system is more than just an anatomical system of nerves and nerve branches and that chemical reactions within the space between the nerves are responsible for triggering information along the nerves' pathways.

If we consider our relatively recent scientific ignorance and the subsequent breakthrough scientific advances, we will realize that we do not yet know it all. There is still much to be learned. I and many other clairvoyant energy system "seers" know that the chakra system and life force system exist within the human body and that the human body does not live without these conscious energy systems. The human body is simply part of a larger system of conscious energy. The chakra system and life force line are these larger energy systems. The chakra system (Figures 1 and 2, chapter 2) is an energy system perfectly designed to fit the human body energetically and functions to link the denser physical body's energy to the energy of the emotions, mind, spirit and soul. The physical body, the chakra system, and the soul or life force line are all energetically compatible and joined in physical human life.

If you will glance at the diagrams of the chakra system and life force line (Figures 1, 2, and 3, chapter 2) you will get a two-dimensional picture of these energy systems. Just as a diagram of the physical body does not capture its dynamic forces, these diagrams do not give you the colors, movement, vibrance, or energy sense of the chakra system or the life force line. These phenomena are only known through experiencing them. That is where we come back to our spiritual energy practices. By practicing meditation, self-examination, and prayer, you will experience the energy systems that are a part of your physical body and joined to your eternal energy self.

The Chakra Energy System

Chapter two only briefly touched on the chakra system. It is difficult to conceptualize a system such as the chakra system if you cannot see it. The wonderful thing about the chakra system and the life force line is that they can be felt and experienced even if you are unable to see them yet. That is why we employ meditation. In meditation you are able to sense, feel, and discover your own chakra system and eventually that of others.

The chakra system is a swirling, moving energy consciousness that grows, develops, and shifts with our own physical, emotional, mindful, and spiritual growth. When the chakra system is healthy and functioning well, it brings healthy life force energy up from the earth into our first chakra and moves that energy through the entire chakra system. Energy flows up from the first chakra through the emotional center (chakra two), to the mental center (chakra three), to the heart center (chakra four), to the throat chakra (chakra five), to the mind's eye (chakra six), to the crown chakra (chakra seven), and on to the Divine. Energy flowing along this chakra course is much more conscious and spiritual than blood flowing through the circulatory system. The flow of energy through the chakra system is the flow of energy of all that we are: our physical life force, our emotional life, our rational mind, our spiritual heart, our spiritual voice, vision and divine energetic connection. The chakra system is a fantastic energetic force that unites the physical to the emotional to the thoughtful to the heartful to the voiceful to the spiritual.

You can see from the diagram that the chakras are arranged in a sequence of one to seven in the body. Though the major chakras line up in the center of the body, we have mini chakras or energy centers all through our bodies. All the chakras are located in specific areas on the human body and have symbolic and energetically meaningful relationships to those areas of the body. However, we must understand that all the chakras work together and all are integrated and interdependent. You cannot simply state that the first chakra has only to do with the legs and genitals. The first chakra is energetically connected to the workings of the entire physical body. Similarly, the second chakra is connected to the emotional center and all emotional life, not just those emotions that are felt in the abdominal region of the body. The same is true of our heart's emotions, the fourth chakra, and our place in the world, the fifth chakra. The seventh chakra holds our spiritual connection to the Divine and opens to the Divine. All the chakras work together as part of our chakra system. They bring *qi* in and through the system and send *qi* out. The chakras bring feelings and thoughts through our energy system, process them, and send them out.

The chakra system channels tornadoes of energy along the primary line of light that beam out and tell the world who we are. This energy changes shades of color, frequency, movement, and function with our moods, physical health, thoughts, actions, and spiritual connection. The chakra system forms the aura around the human body. The colors, vibration, and size of this aura are related to the chakras and how our chakra system is functioning. What we are thinking, feeling, experiencing, and how we feel physically can all be viewed in the aura and chakra system. We are like walking rainbows, and our chakra systems are the rainbow makers.

The chakras themselves are vortices of energy that connect to a primary line of light or life force line, which connects all the chakras through its core line of energy. Within this core line of energy we also have an eternal and core divine essence called the soul. The soul line is linked to the chakra system energetically but represents the most profound aspect of who we are and, as such, is less changeable than the chakras. Though the aura may shift instantly with our thoughts, moods, physical health, or spiritual stance, the soul reflects the less alterable, the deepest sense of who we are in the eternal realms.

In the human life cycle, the physical body, the chakra system, and the life force line are joined and work together harmoniously. The chakra system demonstrates the entire premise for mind-body medicine. Here, in the chakra system we easily see the relationship of body, mind, and spirit from an energetic point of view and can realize that each aspect of our humanness is joined and communicates from, with, and through energy. Our physical bodies receive, process, use, and give out energy; our emotional self, mental self, thoughtful self, and spiritual self do the same, and all these selves do this within the chakra system.

The following chakra acquaintance energy exercise will assist you in experiencing your own chakra system.

Chakra Acquaintance Exercise

This healing exercise is designed to acquaint you with the human energy system commonly referred to as the chakra system. Chakras are spinning vortices of colored light, energy, and vibration, which produce the human aura. Through the practice of energetic meditation, many people develop their spiritual or third eye vision and can begin to see, feel, and sense their own auras and those of others.

For a quick visual review of the chakra system, please refer to the diagrams (pages 14-16, Figures 1, 2, and 3) of the chakra system in chapter 2.

In this exercise, we will begin by attempting to kinesthetically (using the sense of movement) feel the different chakras and the sensations or energies they carry within them.

FIRST CHAKRA   This chakra is located between the legs and attaches to a central line of light that runs up through the body and connects to all the chakras (see Figure 1). The first chakra literally grabs our physical life force and contains our sexuality and our power in the world as physical beings.

A healthy first chakra is a rich red color. This chakra is associated with physical vitality, lust for life, and certainty and security in oneself as a physical being who walks powerfully and confidently upon the earth. If that description made you cringe your first chakra is probably weak. Very few of us have well-developed first chakras, and often those who do are underdeveloped in their other chakras. We are seeking a healthy, balanced chakra system.

To get a feel for your own first chakra stand with your legs a shoulder width apart and slightly bent at the knees. Place your hands on your hips. (If you are unable to stand, sit with your legs spread to the sides, knees bent with your feet on the floor, and your spine upright, and place your hands on your hips.) Rotate your pelvis slightly and feel the power of your open physical connection to the earth. If you are doing this power-stance properly, you will feel energy moving between your legs, up into your genital area, and deep into your pelvis. If this exercise is uncomfortable for you psychologically because it feels too sexual or too power-ful, that in itself gives you information about your own na-ture. We make no judgments, just observations that may assist us here.

SECOND CHAKRA   This is the seat of our first emotions. It is located on the front of the body with a counterpart on the rear of the body (see Figure 1).

This chakra is the place where all human life grows in the womb. It is the chakra that represents our emotional self. This chakra contains our primary emotions or reactions: fear, anxiety, security, self-contentment, etc. The best way to know this chakra is to remember an incident that really frightened you, like a near car accident or a life-threatening event where you felt primal fear. Remember how that fear felt and you will immediately know you felt it first in the pit of your abdomen and then it continued to course upward through you.

The second chakra is a beautiful orange color and like all the other chakras it can be overdeveloped, underdeveloped, scarred, murky, or in any manner dysfunctional. When it is functioning well, it works together in a balanced way with all the other chakras. If we are overly emotional or emotionally repressed, this chakra is not functioning in a balanced man-ner. Of course we all experience times of imbalance in our chakra systems: our energy system is part of our dynamic interaction with life and life events. But some of us have never experienced a balanced emotional center and therefore this chakra is always misaligned or malfunctioning. To feel this chakra, stand or sit in the stance for first chakra and bring your attention (consciousness) to your abdomen and feel for the center of energy within it with your mind and ab-domen. Just note and observe.

THIRD CHAKRA This chakra is located in the solar plexus (see Figure 1) or pit of the stomach. It is the mental chakra, the chakra of the rational mind, which balances thoughts and can suppress, negate, and disregard emotions. It is also the intuitive chakra that feels gut feelings. It is also the chakra that attaches us energetically to our dependent or primary relationships such as those with our parents, siblings, children, husbands, wives, or significant others. If you have ever undergone the trauma of a severed relationship or a painful relationship, you will most likely have felt as if you were stabbed in the stomach with a knife or perhaps you got "sick to your stomach." This, of course, reflects the energetic vibrations or feelings our chakras undergo.

The third chakra is a beautiful yellow and in a culture which values rational thought above all else, it is usually overdeveloped in some aspects and not properly developed in others. To feel this chakra, bring your attention to your stomach area and feel the center of energy within it. The stress-related disorders that have to do with the rational mind and the supression of emotions normally manifest in the area of this chakra. This is the chakra area of ulcers and indigestion.

FOURTH CHAKRA This is the splendid heart chakra. Uplifted into the emotions and spiritual aspects associated with love for others and Divine Spirit, it is situated between the breasts. It is a lovely green color. This is the chakra that loves humanity and God. This is the chakra that modulates the first, second, and third chakras and raises our consciousness to the spiritual realm.

This is the chakra whose heart can be broken through loss of a loved one, whose energy can shrivel and die from sadness or grow brightly and extend out greatly in love and beneficence and embrace the world and others. This is the chakra of heartfelt love. In many, hearts have become closed because of past hurts and injustices or lack of nurturing by the love of an open and beneficent heart chakra. When we feel loved, safe, and secure, our chest area is open, expanded, and full. When we feel guarded, attacked, or unsafe, we protect this area by contracting, pulling in our shoulders, slumping, or simply building an energetic shield or defense through which we will not connect in a heart-vulnerable way with others.

To feel this chakra, bring your attention up to your chest, between your breasts, and sense the point or center of energy there. Note and observe.

FIFTH CHAKRA   This is our voice in the world and our voice to Spirit. It is the place of sound. If you were a sound in the universe, what would it be? Quiet and soft? Loud and raucous? Joyful or sad? Distant and removed? Present and accounted for? This is the chakra that tells who we are to the world and to Spirit.

To feel this blue-colored energy vortex, bring your attention up to the center of your throat, and feel with your mind for the energy center there.

SIXTH CHAKRA   This is the third eye, the seat of your divine vision and the entrance into spiritual sight. It is the eye of clairvoyance. This is the chakra we call the mind's eye. It is your single eye, your spiritual eye. It is the eye that when focused on light, brings light to the entire body. The sixth chakra is a vibrant purple-violet-indigo color. It is the chakra that can be closed to those who do not wish to see with clairvoyant sight or the chakra that can bring magical wonders of spiritual vision to the artist, the dreamer, the prophet, the creative you.

To experience this chakra just be present in consciousness in your mind's eye.

SEVENTH CHAKRA   This is the crown chakra. It is our entrance to Divine Mind and our connection to our Highest Source and the essence of our spiritual nature. Our crown chakra literally opens to heaven. We exit our physical bodies through the crown chakra in death and emerge in the spirit world. We communicate to other realms of existence and

worlds of spirit through this chakra. Often we leave our physical bodies in our dreams and sleep cycles and return again
through this chakra. It is a portal to the life of Spirit. This
chakra is golden-white-silver light. It carries all the colors
of the rainbow within it. It can be opened or closed depending on your own relationship to the Divine.

To feel the seventh chakra, bring your awareness deep
within your mind's eye and up through your crown. If you
are feeling a spiritual connection you will most assuredly feel
an energy concentration at the top of your head.

This simple chakra acquaintance exercise gives you an
internal sense of your chakra system and what it feels like. The
first and seventh chakras are oriented down and up respectively
on the primary line of light and chakras two through six have
front and back complementary chakras.

The chakra system is the energetic life force of the human
body and everyone has one. For many, the chakra system is difficult to understand as an abstract concept. It takes many years of
study to really know human anatomy, physiology, and kinesiol-
ogy, so expecting to understand the chakra system in one quick
easy lesson is improbable. Because it is within you, however, it
can be experienced. The more you practice energy exercises and
meditation exercises, the more you will understand it from a first-
hand kinesthetic experience. Some can see it, some can feel it—
and some cannot.

All physical disease and emotional and spiritual difficulties are present in your energy system oftentimes before they become problems in your life. A well-integrated, smoothly running
energy system can keep your body, mind, and spirit in a healthy
dynamic. This is why energy healers use energy to heal the body.
They are attempting to restore balance and function to the human
energy system and energetically influence the physical body, the
emotional body, and the spiritual body.

In a later chapter, a chakra-balancing exercise will be presented. For now I will explore some examples of dysfunction in
the chakra system and how this system relates to health.

Information Found in the Chakra System

The chakra system, like the human body, carries within it our personal history. The scars we bear from childhood or life incidents that remain as evidence upon our skin are present as well within our chakra system. Chakras can be torn, scarred, ripped, not spinning correctly, relatively closed, too open, or without their protective screen. These descriptions reveal that although chakras are energy, they have an energetic form that can be assessed for healthy functioning, just as the physical body can be.

Our aura, produced by our chakra system, extends around our physical body like a giant egg or cocoon. It is our personal energetic space. When it is violated, we do not feel good. But we can voluntarily mingle our aura with others we desire to be closer to energetically, and this can feel very good. Because the aura blends the energy of all the chakras in a dynamic ever-changing manner, those who can see or feel it have access to much of the information held within each chakra. If a person is ill, his aura will reflect that illness. So, too, will the chakra system. The illness can be seen or felt by one skilled at human energy field assessment. Moods, emotions, and thoughts are also carried in the aura and chakra system and can be seen or felt in either. An energy healer can actually read the aura or chakra system and gather information that includes the history and present state of an individual's physical body, emotions, mind, and spirit. That's a lot of information to gather on meeting with another individual. But that is exactly what you can learn to do when you become adept at understanding and reading the human energy field.

The Chakra System and Health

To see a healthy chakra system is to see all the chakras spinning in a certain direction (normally clockwise in North America), and vibrant in their colors. They are anatomically placed and well connected to the primary life force line. The flow of energy up through the chakras will be strong and balanced through the entire system. Unfortunately, there are not many healthy chakra systems.

Inner and outer life experiences intrude on the well-being of our chakra systems and cause dysfunction, illness, or injury. This can occur on any level or in any area of the chakra system, but will affect the entire chakra system because all the chakras are interrelated and interdependent. For example, if a first chakra is mostly closed it will not bring enough *qi* (life force energy) up into the chakra system and thus will affect the amount of energy the entire system obtains. Other chakras can be thrown out of balance or pulled toward the side to obtain the energy flow they need to function.

How could a first chakra be partially closed? In any number of ways: A child might not have learned that sexuality is healthy or that the physical aspects of a powerful kinesthetic connection to earth are important. There may have been some injury to someone's lust for life or perhaps one lives in an atmosphere that discourages the more physical or earthy embrace of life. Someone could have been ill as a child or suffered some trauma related to the first chakra that resulted in it closing.

There are multitudinous reasons for dysfunctional chakras. The dysfunction often occurs when we are growing up, but can occur at any time in life. We can also have a dysfunction in the chakra system that does not manifest in the physical body for quite some time. For example, a person could have undergone a severance of a relationship that was important to her and subsequently part of her third chakra was torn. It may take many years for this energetic chakra tear—if unrepaired—to develop into a physical problem such as indigestion or an ulcer or food sensitivities.

The above examples demonstrate how life events affect our chakra system. Inner life processing also affects our chakra system. We can cut ourselves off from our first chakra energy. We can cut ourselves off from our emotions. We can cut ourselves off from others. We can cut ourselves off from the Divine. All will show up in the dysfunction of our chakra system. Our chakra system holds no secrets. It shows who we are and where we have been.

At this point you might be thinking that your chakra system is really screwed up. Not so. Fortunately, the chakra system is even more resilient than the human body. It is malleable and readily repairable. How? With energy of course!—the energy of the spiritual disciplines. By practicing the kinesthetic, vibratory, and journeying meditations, you become energy conscious and can access energy and learn to move it through your chakra system. You can use sounding and movement to clear and open the chakras for healthy life force. Through meditation, you become conscious of your chakra system and its flow. Self-examination allows your emotions, thoughts, and mind a healthy flow and expression. Prayer and relationship to Spirit allow chakra energy to flow through its natural progression, earth to sky, and allow you to be what you are—an eternal being in a physical body. As we clear the channels or chakras, we become the energetic bridges between earth and heaven. The three simple spiritual energy disciplines affect the health of our entire chakra system.

A healthy chakra system neither prevents us from undergoing the rigors and difficulties of life nor precludes their influence upon us. What a healthy chakra system does do is allow us to undergo these influences in an energetically balanced way that stretches our bodies, minds, and spirits to grow in strength, wisdom, and knowledge. Our chakra system will age with us as our bodies do. The chakra system contains our physical, emotional, mental, and spiritual aspects and can age in an eloquent, beautiful, and colorful way. There are many vibrant, robust, and healthy chakra systems belonging to geriatric people, and their aged physical bodies reflect the glow of their healthy chakra systems.

The Life Force/Soul Line System

The life force system parallels the line of the chakra system, but it holds the essence of our most permanent self—the soul. This soul line system is our dearest-held sacredness. It reflects the truth of who we are.

This system, discussed in chapter 2, contains the five concentrations of life force energy diagrammed in Figure 3. The life force system connects to the earth (tan tien) through the profound decision of the soul to be in physical reality. The central star of our divine soul's essence is located in the center of the body. Our soul seat is in the cradle of the chest and manifests our soul's desires and longings. The soul's vision to Divine Eminence, The Creator, is through the gate of entrance, and the soul's actual joining of self to the Divine is the star of uniqueness.

The Soul Line and Illumination

If we live in accordance with our deepest spiritual longings and with sacred trust in ourselves, we live according to our soul's truth. We know our way in the world by listening to the voice of our soul. We know our being is connected to God and walk in faith upon the earth certain in that knowledge. We know our eternal reality and are aware of the lessons our soul has come to learn in this place called earth. We can connect in a soul-felt way to others and emanate from our inner soul system the peace, love, and joy with which we embrace our companion souls. This is the description of a person with an illuminated soul line. Most of us can readily admit we might have difficultly with one or two of those attributes. That's okay, that's being human. But the truth is, we all can become illuminated souls. We just have to consciously reach our soul line and see what it can tell us.

If you are able to see, feel, or connect energetically to your own or another's soul line, you can actually see difficulties or perfection there. There can be misalignment, lack of earth connection, blocks, or disruptions. Many soul lines are shrouded around the stars of light or seat of the soul.

Since our soul line is the deepest essence of who we are, it requires our attention and care. But in a world that does not allow for soul caring, we are left wanting, not knowing how to find, follow, and nurture this central soul essence. Fortunately, the three spiritual disciplines can take us to meet our soul and our essence. By clearing the chakra system and opening the channels of kinesthetic clairvoyance within, we can tune into our own soul. Meditation, reflection, and prayer will bring us home to ourselves so that we may clear away the clouds, align with our soul's purpose in this lifetime, see into the Divine within and around, beam out into the world like a star, and know our uniqueness and oneness with the Creator and all fellow souls. We are never alone in our own soul. We are joined and full and resonate the celestial song of our own divinity.

Soul Essence Meditation, Reflection, and Prayer

Once you are consciously present in your soul's life force system meditation, reflection, and prayer are natural. They are functions of the soul. When you bathe in the glorious shining light of the illuminated soul, you are a living prayer, a living meditation, a living reflection of divine essence. It is here in this soul illumination that you discover, uncover, and explode in brilliance your joyful, beneficent, and radiant being. It is enormously healing for the body, mind, and spirit. For it is perfect love and that is the force that heals all. Let us get to our souls and become one with our own truth. In this lies all true healing through any lifetime. A loving moment in one's own soul can heal the hurts of many things past.

Soul Life-Force-Line Consciousness Exercise

Sit quietly in your place of meditation, reflection, and prayer. Ground and center your energy to the earth and gently close your eyes and breathe in a relaxed manner, in through your nose and out through your mouth.

As you continue your relaxed and deep breathing, bring your consciousness to a deep place within your mind's eye. See there pearlescent gates that open into a crystalline line of moving energy. Bring your consciousness down this line of energy to a place of connection deep within the earth. Stay here a moment and feel your soul's life force in its connection to the earth. Is it soft and sweet, full and forceful, or hesitant and faltering? Hold your stance here and remember why you came into this physical life. Feel the sweetness of the earth's soil as it touches your soul and embraces your presence. Reaffirm your connection to this life and your presence in it. Breathe in the force for life your soul makes in marriage to the earth.

When you feel filled with soulful life force move your awareness up through the tan tien in your pelvis and once again feel your direct life force connection to the earth. Feel its solidness and comfort in the relationship between your body and the earth. Move up toward your central star of being, deep within the core of your body above your navel and below your third chakra. Go within this central star of your own being and feel its brilliant light and radiation. Become one with it and expand your consciousness out like a star from the center of your body. Feel the joy and lightness your expansion creates within you. Grow bright and large; fill the room with your beams of light. Stay in this brilliant radiance and rest completely in beauty.

Now move your awareness up toward the wings of your soul that rest upon your chest. Immerse yourself in the seat of your soul and feel your longings, your desires, your heartfelt dreams. Let them well up within you and fill you with their sweet voice. Stay awhile here and be with your soul.

When full of your soul's beauty, dreams, and longings, move your consciousness up toward the gates of entrance to ascend toward the Divine. Listen for the song of spirit, the call of the supernal light to which you ascend, and come in prayer and love to the place in which your soul was birthed. Rest here awhile in the peace of total love. Bask in the comfort of the one perfect love.

When nurtured and rested and ready to return, gently call your awareness back into your place of meditation and prayer. Open your eyes, sigh, stretch, and bask in the wonderful feeling of your alive and radiant soul, rooted in the vessel of your body.

Illness and the Energy Systems

The energy systems of the human body, the chakra system, and the life force line encompass all that we are as humans. Body, mind, and spirit are truly joined through these energy systems and health is possessed by all three systems on a continuum that joins body and spirit. These are dynamic energy systems and have an effect on one another. If we have a physical illness, it most certainly manifests itself in our chakra system and aura. It does not necessarily appear on the soul life force line because this line reflects the divine and eternal essence of the self. However, our soul line, if kept apart from our consciousness or ignored or defied, can cause illness in the chakra system and physical body.

We cannot take an illness and ascribe it to one cause. There are too many variables and too many causes. The body could simply have been polluted or overwhelmed by a life-taking vibration (bacteria, virus, cancer), or an unhealthy chakra system could be unable to assist in warding off disease, or a soul that is unheard and unhappy might have little life force to sustain it. These same variables apply to all dysfunctions and illnesses of the body, mind, or spirit. We can respond to dysfunction by gathering our own resources and drawing upon the resources of science and medicine to work toward health. Wellness and life force energy in all the systems will work toward sustaining health. But we must remember that there will be a time to leave the physical body. A functional chakra system and a soul-conscious spirit will make the transition one of peace and comfort. Therefore, it is in our best interest to keep all our energy systems healthy.

The Spiritual Disciplines and Our Energy Systems

We needn't memorize the pathways of the body, chakra system, and the soul line systems to begin to learn how to harness life force and assist in opening and clearing our energy systems. Simply by practicing the three spiritual energy disciplines we will begin to actively heal all the energy systems. This healing is a learning process and the best way to learn is by doing.

If you practice these disciplines, your energy centers will move toward alignment and healthy functioning. The clouds around your soul line will drift away, and your soul will illuminate your consciousness. Your body will resonate with increased energy and ability to recover from and fight illness. By combining the spiritual disciplines and nurturing the body with healthy foods, fluids, exercise, fresh air, sunlight, and rest, you will give all the energy systems optimal opportunity to restore health. Many physical illnesses are due solely to lack of the above health and life force–enhancing practices. There is much of the earth that facilitates healing of the body, much of the mind that heals the body, mind, and spirit, and much of the spirit that heals all.

Chapter 6

✳

BODY, MIND, AND SPIRIT MEDICINE

Because we are beings whose form and essence comprise physical, emotional, mental, and spiritual dimensions, we need to pay attention to our health in all of these dimensions. This means that if we have a physical complaint or illness we need to look for physical reasons for our complaint. The fact that many physical illnesses and complaints are now generally thought to be stress-related, lifestyle-related, or psychologically influenced does not preclude the fact that there are real physical manifestations of our health complaints and real physical disease-causing agents in our environment. Traumatic accidents, injuries, occupational hazards, pollution, toxic carcinogens, poor sanitary and hygienic conditions, and a host of viruses, bacteria, genetic diseases, and disease processes exist in the world as a part of daily life.

In the scope of body, mind, and spirit medicine what is most essential is the impact that a physical, emotional, mental, or spiritual health complaint has on all dimensions of our being. It is not beneficial, therapeutic, or clinically responsible to assume that if we have a physical complaint, disease, or injury that we somehow caused it by a "wrong-thinking" mind or because we have a spiritual sickness that is now manifesting itself physically. Of course we can have physical conditions that originate in or are exacerbated in the mental or spiritual dimension of our existence, but to judge all diseases or injuries in this manner is not to partake of the highest realm of body, mind, and spirit medicine.

All human life is sacred and all human soul journeys through this physical life are part of a complex and intimate relationship between the soul and Divine Spirit. This being so, no one can judge why someone gets a sickness and someone else does not, why someone has a tragic accident and someone else does not, or why catastrophes occur to some and not to others. What can be done and is most beneficial to do is to lead or assist a fellow human being to optimal wellness in all dimensions of health and to allow the soul journey to unfold sacredly and intimately within the dimensions of that individual's own life path.

I speak of this here because much of the appropriate criticism aimed at mind-body medicine is for the glibness and superficiality of the quick judgment that if someone is sick or the victim of tragic circumstances that somehow that individual caused the problem by practicing poor spiritual and mindful practices. This is not for anyone to decide. This is not the only truth. There are many good, brave, and beloved brothers and sisters who undergo what is terrible and tragic and are examples to others of highly evolved spiritual beings in human form. The human form is temporary and the lessons of the soul eternal. As a human I dare not in the darkness of my own ignorance judge another soul's divine course. We can draw upon the fountain of information available regarding body, mind, and spirit medicine, but let us remain awestruck and humble before the divine nature of Spirit and the possibilities of that which we do not know.

We can learn much about what is healing and health maintaining by looking at what we do know. We live with a marvel of modern scientific advances that can help diagnose, heal, or prolong physical life on the earth. We have what is called western medicine and what is called alternative medicine. Both systems have treatments for the body and mind. Western medicine has physiological medicine and psychiatric/psychological medicine. Alternative medicine has those as well as spiritual healing. Both medical traditions offer wonderful ways for healing and maintaining health. Individuals who are ill should seek assistance from the tradition or traditions that are best prepared to help them. This could mean combining western medicine with alternative medicine or utilizing one exclusive of the other depending on the nature of the problem.

But what are the offerings of each and how do you discern which is most beneficial? Educate yourself: learn *what* is available and make a choice based on personal trial and error to decide what works.

Western Medicine and Alternative Medicine

Both western medicine and alternative medicine exist to heal the sick and suffering and to promote health. Western medicine traditionally devotes its knowledge and practice to healing physical complaints with physical interventions and agents including medications, drugs, chemicals, surgery, and physical manipulations of the body. There are miraculous modern diagnostic tools and devices for finding disease or injury in the body. Among these are blood tests, urine and sputum cultures, X rays, CAT scans, MRIs, physical assessment and observation, and clinical findings that correlate to specific disease processes or injuries. The advances of western medicine in treating the physical body are truly admirable, gratifying, and necessary.

Western medicine comprises a host of specialty areas that cover all parts of the body and phases of disease processes or injuries. The professionals who work in the western medical system are required to have licensure and certification in their areas of practice and are mandated to have undergone academic and clinical training within accredited institutions. A universal language of the body has been established to describe standard anatomy, physiology, and pathology. Physicians, nurses, physician's assistants, technologists, pharmacists, technicians, nutritionists, physical therapists, occupational therapists, speech pathologists (each with his respective field of expertise) are joined in a megasystem designed to treat the ailing human body.

Western medical tradition also offers treatment to psychologically or mentally challenged individuals. There is even a system of social services designed to address the social and psychological needs of the American population. Western medicine certainly attempts to address the needs of its clients and has a tremendous regulated system of care designed for that purpose. So why has there been such an increase in the number of people who visit and spend their health care dollars on services provided by alternative medicine practitioners? Even the American Medical Association would like to know the answer to this question. There are many reasons, but we will explore the most obvious first.

"Alternative medicine" is an umbrella term for a diverse group of healing practices and theories. Alternative medicine includes, but is not limited to, acupuncture, biofeedback, energy field therapy or laying on of hands, homeopathy, herbal medicine, manual healing and neuromuscular therapies, nutrition and diet regimens, bioelectromagnetic treatments, and a host of other mind-body-spirit healing practices. Like western medicine, alternative medicine addresses physical illnesses. The one common denominator in all of alternative medicine's varied treatment and healing offerings is the basic acceptance that body and mind are inexorably joined in health and in both the disease and healing processes. That the American/western population is now utilizing the services of practitioners of alternative medicine in large numbers demonstrates that many people agree with this assumption.

Western medicine is unable to meet the total health-care needs of the population for many reasons. Not all disease is treatable by western medical means, and the megasystem itself does not always provide for treating the human being who shows up physically ill as more than a physical entity. This does not negate the fact that there are many dedicated individuals within the western medical system who truly care for their patients as whole beings; it just reports with honesty the fact that the western medical system is not based on the theoretical construct that the body and mind are joined in health and illness. Furthermore, the western medical system is drowning in crippling costs and has reduced time and services to patients as a result. There is neither the time, money, or energy to treat more than the body. There are individuals who will do so, but if the complaint is strictly physical, health-care professionals are not reimbursed for addressing the whole person.

Practitioners of alternative medicine fill this gap. For the most part their services are affordable to the average health-care consumer, who most often is willing to pay cash. Additionally, the length of time a practitioner of alternative medicine spends one-on-one with a client or patient is considerably longer than that spent by a practioner of western medicine. During this time, attention is directly focused on the patient for an uninterrupted period. Human beings who are suffering, confused, and in need of help appreciate the devotion of time and concern to their body and mind.

Cost and attention are two reasons the population seeks out alternative medicine practitioners, but there are many other reasons. Many of alternative medicine's practices have shown demonstrable healing results for the population that has used them. If alternative medicine wasn't successful to some degree, people wouldn't use it.

All the practices that fall under the alternative medicine umbrella are not without problems and some valid questions have been raised about them. Who are these practitioners and what are their credentials? Because the term alternative medicine is so broad and all-encompassing, how do you regulate it? Where is the accountability of the practitioners? Should their services be reimbursed by health insurance? These questions are timely and legitimate.

Fortunately, inroads are being made in this area by the establishment of the National Institutes of Health Office of Alternative Medicine. There are also many health-care providers who are trained in western medicine and are alternative medicine practitioners as well. The bridging of these two traditions with research, a common language, and a willingness on both sides to expand their field of knowledge will most certainly enhance health-care provision in this era.

I ardently believe that any alternative medicine practitioner who touches or influences the body in any manner must have a working knowledge of human anatomy, physiology, and pathology and/or work in cooperation with these who do have these credentials. The same can be said for alternative practitioners who work with the human mind and spirit. A thorough foundation in psychology or psychotherapeutics is essential as is cooperation with individuals who possess this knowledge. Western medical practitioners, too, can stretch their boundaries to become educated in the practices of alternative medicine. There will always be the need for specialists and interdisciplinary teamwork in health and healing. Advances will be made with cooperation and devotion to the best possible health and healing methods.

Finding Appropriate Care

In seeking health care for ourselves as integrated physical, mental, and spiritual beings we need to know exactly what is available and how we as individuals can use these two health-care systems. We do not abandon common sense and good judgment when we view ourselves as spiritual beings in human form: we heighten our common sense and good judgment. If I were having a heart attack, I would rush to the nearest emergency room rather than seek out an alternative medicine practitioner unless she was also an emergency physician with all the equipment and medication needed to save my life at that moment. Afterward I might consult an alternative practitioner if I wished to find out if my lifestyle affected my predisposition to a heart attack or if the heart attack was related to stress or diet or any number of physical, mental, and spiritual issues.

In any given situation I most certainly am going to avail myself of the immediate care needed. But with physical, mental, and spiritual awareness, I am also going to remember to treat myself as a whole being. All physical health complaints impact upon the mind and spirit just as all mental and spiritual complaints eventually affect the body. The body, mind, and spirit are interdependent and interrelated until the death of the physical form. Knowing this, I always seek appropriate healing on all levels of my being.

Both western and alternative medicine offer physical healing agents for the body. Alternative medicine has techniques and methods that act as powerful agents upon the body. Just as one would be concerned about the potency and side effects of a prescription drug or about the trauma of surgery, one should be concerned about the effects of all physical agents and interventions used in alternative medicine. Just because something is called alternative medicine does not mean it's gentle or benign. Herbal treatments, physical body manipulation, diet and nutrition regimens, and so on have physical impact on the body. These are not necessarily benign agents. Herbs can cause toxicity as can medication; physical manipulation can be performed in an unskilled manner, and diets and nutritional regimens can starve or kill the body. Consumer beware both of western medicine and alternative medicine. Responsible, educated, and accountable practitioners exist in both medical traditions. So do frauds: irresponsible, uneducated, and unethical practitioners.

Preventive Care

Both western and alternative medicine practitioners espouse preventive health care or wellness practices. Proper diet, avoidance of health risk factors, proper or healthy lifestyle choices, and regular physical exercise are recommended for the human body's health. Alternative medicine practitioners would further recommend mental and spiritual exercises for the wellness of the physical body. In the circle of life, we would do well to always embrace nourishing and health-maintaining practices for the body, mind, and soul as well as to minimize our susceptibility to physical illness or injury by maintaining healthy immune systems and strong musculoskeletal systems and cardiovascular systems that consistently ward off disease and injury.

However, in reality, most people do not live this way, and even those who do may experience illness or injury. This being the case, it serves us to have a deeper understanding of the temporal nature of the body and to grasp the opportunities for learning that a physical illness or injury presents to us. Obviously, I am speaking of the mental and spiritual lessons the body can bring us whether in sickness or health. No one medical system has all the answers to curing life-challenging illnesses, progressive physical diseases, or traumatic physical injury. The path toward health appears to be in utilizing the gifts of both western and alternative medicine and in addressing the needs of the body, mind, and spirit with self-healing practices.

There are ways to enhance any western medical treatment with mind-body medicine to facilitate healing and the quality of life. Some disease processes respond well to mind-body interventions, and many people who live with disease and injury attain a more comfortable and life-affirming plane of consciousness through their attention to themselves as spiritual beings. When we live to the fullest level of spiritual, mental, and physical wellness, we may shift our perception of what total health truly is. We are physical, mental, and spiritual beings and our health depends upon addressing ourselves as such. We need to practice those activities that will bring increased health to the body, mind, and spirit.

Body, Mind, and Spirit Medicine and Energy Healing Techniques

The linking of western medicine and alternative medicine is the new frontier. As a practitioner in both medical traditions, I have seen the two work well together to assist in healing. To illustrate how traditional western and alternative medicine practices can be joined to assist in healing, I will present some examples of healing efforts that combined both traditions.

My expertise in alternative medicine is in the area known as energy healing. Please remember that although I am a healer who can see inside the body through the aura and chakra system and therefore can see disease, illness, or problems therein, any individual can become aware of his or her own aura, chakra system, and body by practicing the spiritual energy disciplines. So though I may recount examples where I as a healer diagnosed, influenced, or assisted in healing someone else's ailment, each of us can cultivate many of these same healing abilities to assist in her own healing.

I do not do my healing work alone. I have spiritual guides who direct me in my healing work. You do, too. We all have wise souls who are with us to assist us in life and who do not reside in a human body. We become aware of our spirit guides through our spiritual energy practices. These beneficent and loving souls have energetic hands to bring healing energy to your life force system and physical body. In meditation, prayer, and reflection they are with you. Invite their healing energy, and it will be with you.

Relieving Pain with Energy

Once I treated a client who was diagnosed with cancer in the advanced stages. The cancer had spread throughout his body and had invaded his kidneys, bones, and lungs. He had not been given very long to live and medically no treatment was going to heal him. This gentle soul was not a complainer and when his pain became so intense that he could not leave his room, I became disconcerted and upset. He was living in a nursing home where there were regulations regarding the use of narcotics, which meant that he could not be given morphine for his pain.

This was a man who knew how to pray and was quite ready to die. He just wanted the pain to be lessened. Unable to change the medication regulations, I decided to use energy therapy techniques. At this stage of his illness, I was not about to try to teach him how to meditate. I had to give him the meditative energy.

And so we began healing energy work. The client's deepest wish was to have his pain lessened enough to fall asleep each evening and that is what I used the healing energy for. I would place my hands over the area of his greatest source of pain and run soothing, anesthetizing energy through my hands and into his body and energy field. He would drift off to sleep, and I would softly leave the room.

This sweet and gentle man passed to the spirit world in his sleep, but not before he taught me a great lesson about dying with dignity, grace, and honor.

Energetic Interventions to Prevent Premature Birth

I received a distressing phone call from my youngest sister one evening. Diane was twenty-eight weeks pregnant with her third child and had begun to show signs and symptoms of early labor. She was having premature contractions and her cervix was dilated. That day Diane had been to her obstetrician who informed her that she was three to four centimeters dilated and she would have to limit her activities to bed rest to avoid a possible premature delivery. Diane had two other small children at home, and complete bed rest was, of course, a ridiculous joke.

Diane's situation was emotionally and psychologically complicated by the memories of her second child's premature delivery and birth. This child had been delivered four weeks early and was gravely ill at birth. The physicians had given Diane very poor odds for the child's survival and the likelihood that its physical impairments might be sustained. This child recovered miraculously with no physical defects, but that is another miraculous healing story. In this moment Diane was remembering the past and now she was only seven months pregnant. My youngest sister was deeply afraid. I drove to Diane's house and saw her on her living room couch. Diane knows of my energy healing work and agreed to what I told her I was going to do energetically to her first chakra and cervix.

I placed my hands between my sister's legs as she lay back on the couch. Her clothes were on. Energy passes through clothing. I directed energy up through the first chakra and gently sewed a series of energetic loops through the tip of the cervix. I then gently sent energy through the uterus to relax it and cease the contractions.

I also talked spiritually to the baby to tell her it wasn't time yet. This conversation occurred on the soul line level, and the baby had a choice in the matter. She decided to stay awhile longer in the nurturance of the womb and continue to develop there.

Diane's premature contractions stopped almost immediately following this energy healing. Diane returned to her obstetrician within the week to be informed that her cervix was now only two centimeters dilated. She continued to follow the bed rest schedule as much as she was able until her delivery date which was at her full forty weeks.

The warning that energy work or alternative medicine techniques are not always benign is certainly applicable here. Diane went through a very long labor and had difficulty dilating her cervix. She was given medication to speed up her labor and cervical dilation because of this. When she went into labor, I hadn't yet released the energetic stitches that held her cervix closed. I was not mindful that this would be necessary. Thankfully I realized this after some time and prayed and consciously sent energy to her energy field to release the energetic sutures. Additionally, Diane and the baby's own energy fields were pushing toward birth, and just as silk stitches would have released under that pressure, so would the energetic stitches. Baby and mother were just fine. I am very grateful that Diane lovingly recalls my assistance in preventing premature birth and not my assistance in prolonging her labor.

Healing Energy in Conjunction with Western Medicine

The above two energy healing stories demonstrate that energy healing techniques can be used in conjunction with traditional western medicine. In both cases, the clients were being treated by the western medical system. Energy healing was used to augment their treatment protocols and assist the clients in health complaints that required attention. In both situations additional traditional western medical treatments could have been implemented. The pain of the cancer could have been treated with morphine or other pain-relieving medications. Diane might have had to undergo more extensive medical interventions and monitoring if her premature labor signs had not abated. Energy healing relieved the symptoms in both instances. If energy healing had not worked, further traditional western medicine methods could have been employed.

Participating in Healing Ourselves

These examples also show the intervention of an energy healer. However, when we learn about our own energy fields and receive guidance on how to utilize healing energy effectively, we can do much to assist in our own healing. Energy healing can be learned to some degree by all people. Of course there are times when we need physicians, health-care providers, and alternative healers. However, there are many preventive care measures and healing exercises we can learn to empower our self-healing ability. New information regarding biofeedback and pain management shows that many people can modify their levels of pain with meditation. Additionally, people with chronic illnesses can learn energy conservation techniques and adapt their lifestyles to support more comfortable and health assuring circumstances.

Body, mind, and spirit medicine looks at all aspects of illness and health. In energy field healing, individuals have the opportunity to look within their own energy systems, learn the possible difficulties therein, and foster healing through the spiritual energy disciplines of meditation, self-examination, and prayer. Once you have a basic understanding of the human body, the chakra system, and the life force soul line, you can harness the energy of earth, self, and Spirit to assist you in healing.

The Educated Consumer

In both alternative medicine and traditional western medicine, the more we as health consumers know about our illnesses and treatment options, the better equipped we are to participate in our own recovery. This approach to health care is called patient education. Learning as much as you can about the problem and methods of treatment gives you as a patient more power in healing yourself. You are empowered by knowledge.

To learn about the health-care options available, you must gather information and become an educated consumer. I am not an expert in herbal treatment remedies or in nutrition; however, there are many books on those subjects and if I felt that these two areas of knowledge would assist my return to health, I would read about them and speak to those who are well-versed in these subjects.

Following Through

Become an active participant in your own healing. Half the battle in healing, whether with western or alternative medicine, is following through on health-facilitating regimens. These regimens include anything from taking medications as prescribed, to doing home exercise programs, to adopting healthier lifestyle options. In energy healing, that means learning and practicing the energy healing disciplines which were explored in chapters 2, 3, and 4.

In chapter 8, I will present some basic energy healing exercises. They are introductory in nature and designed to foster awareness of your own energy field with simple energy healing techniques. They are not designed to take the place of professional health care.

We need to have those among us who are experts in their areas of knowledge. Most of us take our cars to a mechanic for major problems, but we certainly benefit from a working knowledge of how our cars work and our cars benefit from preventive maintenance like regular oil changes or replacing spark plugs. Our bodies, minds, and spirits are certainly more important to us than our cars. A basic understanding of how they work, how they are running, and how to perform regular energy tune-ups benefits our health and well-being.

Emotions, Thoughts, and Illness

As you can plainly see in the chakra system diagram (Figure 2), all our energy centers are connected. Therefore our emotions and thoughts or mental attitude can affect our physical health and well-being.

When I am constantly stressed, upset emotionally, or having obsessive worrisome thoughts, I get physically ill. My body tells me to slow down by the swelling of glands in my neck or a bout of gastrointestinal distress. I get this message early now, because I am aware of my own energy field and know that my emotional and mental life affect my physical body. This doesn't mean I can avoid these messages entirely. After all, I am a human being who gets caught up in trying to make a living, struggling with household chores, dealing with people every day, and trying to be in significant relationships with those I love. In the midst of all of this, I can stop doing what is good for my body, mind, and spirit, and the result is that I become ill.

This is true for many of us: we each have a red flag in our physical body that pops up to say "Hi, you are bent out of shape and I'm not going to work anymore!" When you are aware of the way your body, mind, and spirit are joined, you will not ignore this red flag. I don't. I take a day off. I turn off the telephone and do what I need to do to get my health in order. I address the red flag and pay attention. I remember to rest, eat well, and meditate. I process my thoughts and feelings through self-examination and prayer. I energetically assist my recovery and hope to remember to regularly employ health-maintenance activities for my body, mind, and spirit to remain well.

Many of us have chronic or life-long predispositions to specific physical difficulties that are related to our emotions and thoughts. Body, mind, and spirit medicine recognizes this truth and promotes the wellness activities of self-examination, meditation, and prayer to assist in healing these conditions by discovering the trigger or triggers, learning and practicing energy healing disciplines, and preventing recurrence through healthier energetic alternatives.

Spiritual Disease and Illness

Our relationship to self and Spirit can also foster illness or health. Those things we consider as spiritual in nature—love, relationships to others and God—can bring us physical, emotional, mental, and spiritual discord if our inner life is filled with unresolved guilt, anger, bereavement, or bitterness. If we suppress, deny, and refuse to engage in our inner spirit's feelings and thoughts, we can also manifest disease of the body, mind, or spirit. Cutting ourselves off from our spirit's urgings or needs results in damage. We can develop physical complaints, mental illnesses, or spirit sickness, from lack of self-love. Our spirit needs to be nurtured and given sustenance through regular energy practices.

In body, mind, and spirit medicine, we see that illness can develop in any dimension of the self and requires attention in all dimensions. Dysfunction or difficulty in the body, mind, or spirit can and will affect the functioning of our whole being. That is why we address all we are to heal in order to stay healthy. Not only can we heal the specific illness, we can prevent its recurrence and maintain a more dynamic, healthy balance among all of our energy systems.

Body, Mind, and Spirit Medicine in Life's Purpose

The "magic" that can happen to us in any dimension of our health by practicing physical, mental, and spiritual wellness is no magic at all. It is the larger reality of our eternal nature of being and our own innate power to heal ourselves. Drugs, surgery, qi practices, herbs, diet, movement, energy, meditation, and psychotherapy are purely energetic/vibrational interventions that serve to teach us about our multidimensionality and our responsibility to our health on all levels.

Ultimately, unless the human body can serve the spirit it is of no use to us. The things to which the body clings that are solely of the material plane will not bring us anything of lasting value. The body does return to the earth. If the body is joined to the mind and spirit to gather those lessons and opportunities for the soul to evolve, the cells of every physical system are imbued with divine essence even in illness and injury. The human life cycle then renders itself purposeful in the attainment of wisdom and spiritual growth. Let us seek those things that bring us increased health on all levels of our being with the awareness that our very nature is eternal and connected to the Divine Creator.

The principles of body, mind, and spirit medicine can always be incorporated into our daily lives. We can treat our physical illnesses and injuries with all the artillery at our command. All things of the world can serve Divine Spirit. Therefore all medical treatments, all human interactions, and all activities can serve Divine Spirit to heal the self. Having spiritual practices that bring enlightenment, inner wisdom, and guidance will steer you on the path to your own health. When you view all things and yourself as energy/vibrational systems you will be very discerning as to what you will or will not allow into your system. You will be far more able to assess the advantages or disadvantages of any health-care treatment and its consequences on your total being. So, in effect, your own spiritual practices can guide you in wellness, illness, prevention, and healing. By performing these life-enhancing disciplines, you will walk in the world with an intuitive sense of what you need for healing and what you need for soul development and joy.

When the physical body aches and the soul is weary, we are in need of healing. With our emerging awareness of body, mind, and spirit, let us tend to all that we are. Meet the body's requirements for healing through your entire consciousness. Gifted souls abound in the healing and medical arts. Find them and follow your internal voice in finding that which is offered for healing in this world. I have stated that both western and alternative medicine can be used conjointly to improve the body's ability to heal itself. This is true and easily fits the model of body, mind, and spirit medicine. If the life force is waning or under attack by disease, then we must use all agents available to restore health and vitality to the life force and eradicate the human energy eaters from the body. Restoration of life force involves all those human activities that soothe and create greater positive life force in the body, mind, and spirit. Negative forces that do not serve to promote positive life force can be surgically removed, chemically treated, starved, absorbed, digested, and neutralized by healthy life force.

The process of healing is not solely to destroy disease or repair injury; it includes restoring healthy life force to all energy systems of the body/mind/spirit continuum and is a process of balances. We know, for instance, that many of the drugs used to kill disease also kill the healthier cells of the body. We need to pay attention to this and cleanse toxins from the body and boost the life force in creating healthy cells to assist the body in restoring balance. This is achieved on all dimensions of the human energy system. Adequate hydration and nutritional life force techniques for body, mind, and spirit assist the process of cleansing toxins and rejuvenating life force within our energy systems.

Life force techniques that assist in body, mind, and spirit healing can be shared by one human life force with another. Touch, massage, acupuncture, neuromuscular techniques, and energy field therapy are all life force generators that can serve the body, mind, and spirit. Who, when ill, does not require loving physical contact directed toward supporting and restoring her life force? These are real vibratory forces that influence the healing and restoration of the body, mind, and spirit. So are those activities that bring solace, comfort, and rest to the body, mind, and spirit. Music, song, dance, poetry, art, sunshine, the ocean, the mountains, fresh air, solitude, delicious nourishing foods, baths, swing sets, laughter, and play affirm the life force and bring joy. The process for healing involves all that will create increased life force within the self. All the tools of medicine and the mind and the spirit are employed as needed to heal the self.

There are those physical diseases or injuries that cannot be fully eradicated or repaired. Yet we can continue to attempt to heal. Adaptability to circumstance and the creative force of will allows those with physical challenges to achieve great works in all realms of human life. Through combined use of all that is available in western and alternative medicine, physical disease can be slowed, and people can learn to live with their disease in increased comfort and with less physical pain as they accomplish the work of the soul in this human life journey.

The struggle for wholeness of being and connection to the true self is most certainly a sacred soul journey. Even for those who are leaving the human life cycle through illness, the journey of self continues. If we connect to our own deepest self and the divinity within, this journey from physical form to greater reality is simply a transit from earth to sky.

The doorway to other realms of spirit is filled with eternal life force and beauty. Vibrant color, vibrant spirit, and deeper more fulfilling relationships to fellow souls and Loving Spirit await. Life continues past the awareness of the physical realm. So let us be prepared for our transit prior to our leaving. Let us embrace the physical earth *qi* to which we have access.

We are in physical form for a purpose that serves our mind and spirit. We can embrace all that fire and passion of human form and direct it to serve the greater energy of our soul. We can seek to heal, to do our good work in this world, and to find the love within and without.

All health complaints of the body, mind, and spirit can be addressed by what already exists within the world and within ourselves. True healing is not of the body, for the body is temporary at best, but a comfortable life force-filled body can be a wonderful home and joy-producing vessel for the mind and spirit. Therefore, let us remember to nurture and care for our bodies as well as our minds and spirits so that we may evolve the soul, and the human life cycle will have served us well.

The Place of Miracles

We come upon the place of miracles and that which is considered extraordinary when we enter body, mind, and spirit medicine. Like many others who practice body, mind, and spirit medicine, I know that miracles are natural and regular occurrences in the realm of spirit. When they physically manifest themselves, they are seen as exceptional, as unexplainable—as miracles! But they are not exceptional or extraordinary; they are really just the manifestations of Divine Spirit.

The miraculous exists in abundance within and without. Becoming miracle-minded is the gift of soul connection to the Divine Creator. I see miracles everywhere. I do not attempt to classify miracles as of greater or smaller nature. Who is to say that a soul finding peace is a greater or lesser miracle than "curing" an "incurable" physical disease? Not I, for I have seen miracles in abundance and know that a miracle is just what a miracle is—the hand of God touching our consciousness and reminding us of his existence and our true nature.

The body, mind, and spirit practices of meditation, self-examination, and prayer open the path for miracles to occur. These expressions of divine love can more easily come through a clear, conscious prayerful channel. Miracles become the natural order of things when life is viewed through the eyes of a soul who sees all things as connected to God. Life becomes one continuous beholding of miracles. In healing the self, we become channels of the miraculous and extenders of this supernal love.

Body, mind, and spirit medicine calls forth the miraculous. We are one with the Divine Creator, and all life of the earth emanates from him. We become miracle-minded or miracle conscious through spiritual practices that allow us to see with new vision the unfolding moment in a God-connected world. In this vision all things are possible and all healing exists.

Chapter 7

✳

HEALING STORIES

The following healing stories are presented as vignettes from the life journeys of people or patients I have encountered, worked with, or had relationships with, whether personal or professional. All the accounts are true. Confidentiality is sacred to me. In all cases, these healing stories use fictional names. The characters or circumstances may be altered to protect the anonymity of my clients or loved ones, however, the essential or important elements of the healing stories are unchanged.

First, so that you will understand what I am professionally, I will briefly explain to you what an occupational therapist (OT) is and what my healing practice involves.

Occupational Therapy

The word "occupation" refers to the use of goal-oriented activities as part of the therapeutic intervention occupational therapists provide. Occupational therapy's academic/educational foundation links physical and psychosocial studies. The core curriculum includes all the basic biological sciences as well as human anatomy, human physiotherapeutic interventions, and rehabilitation. In addition, occupational therapists have an academic foundation in human psychology including developmental psychology, pathology and disease, and therapeutic psychosocial intervention as related to functioning in daily life. As part of their academic training, occupational therapists are required to do

104

clinical work of various kinds throughout their education. This culminates in an academic year of full-time clinical rotations including both a physical dysfunctional setting and a psychiatric or psychosocial dysfunctional setting. Occupational therapists then can choose specialty areas or become general practitioners in either physical dysfunction, psychosocial dysfunction, or both. As in many medical professions, occupational therapy has very specific specialty areas. The physical dysfunction specialties include pediatric, geriatric, cognitive/head trauma, hand therapy, burn therapy, acute care, long-term care, etc. The psychosocial specialties include addiction/recovery, acute inpatient, chronic outpatient, community-based services, and all areas related to the development of psychosocial skills to improve function in activities of daily living. Within each of these specialties there are OTs who are certified in special training related to their particular area of expertise. Because there are so many specialties, there are, of course, experts in each given field. All OTs possess the same academic background and continue clinical and academic training in specialty areas.

Occupational therapists work in hospitals, schools, psychiatric institutions, nursing homes, private practice, and any clinical setting where rehabilitation is an essential part of the institution or framework. Whether dealing with physical dysfunction or psychiatric dysfunction, we are included on the rehabilitation team along with physical therapists, speech therapists, physicians, nurses, and psychologists. But what exactly is it that occupational therapists do that is different from physical therapists, speech therapists, or other rehab specialists? The best way to describe what we do is to give an example.

In a pediatric setting, an occupational therapist may be presented with a child who demonstrates poor learning skills in school. This child may or may not have a blatant physical problem. The occupational therapist will perform a comprehensive evaluation of this child's developmental motor/sensory skills, cognitive perceptual skills, and psychosocial skills using batteries of tests or assessments geared toward each of those areas. The findings may indicate that the child is mildly developmentally delayed in all areas.

It is the occupational therapist's job to intervene on the child's behalf. Occupational therapists use activities of daily life or occupational activities to promote function for the child. This means employing all the activities that a child needs to master to pass through the normal sequence of neurological, physical, cognitive, and psychosocial stages of development. This might mean that we will position or posture a child in a specific way to train the neuro-musculature or central nervous system through appropriate developmental sequences (for example, prone to supine to quadruped to kneel, etc.) while also addressing the cognitive or perceptual or fine motor skills that are lacking by using play activities or school activities. We will use pictures, writing, peg boards, and so on to promote skill acquisition in those areas. This is a very simple example of an occupational therapist's role in a pediatric setting. Therapy is ongoing, especially in the pediatric population, and will vary with the severity of dysfunction or level of developmental delay. Neonatal OTs work in the earliest developmental setting and once again influence the central nervous system and developmental systems of an infant to stimulate age-appropriate responses or to promote normalized development.

A hospital setting with an acute population also includes specialty areas. There are occupational therapists who work strictly with burn patients. OTs have been very involved in fabricating and using pressure garments to reduce scarring. They also work to prevent contractures by using activities to promote range of motion (movement) to arms, legs, and the entire body and by providing activities that are a part of daily life and require use of the body. These might include toileting, transferring in and out of bed, dressing, and self-care skills.

Occupational therapists also make things. We make splints or orthotics for hands, arms, and the body to facilitate healing, or movement of the body to prevent deformity. Occupational therapists are experts on positioning the human body for activities of daily living. This might include helping someone in a wheelchair or ensuring an ergonomically correct working environment. Occupational therapists in geriatric settings often design and adapt daily products needed by their clients to ensure increased independence in activities of daily living. A person who is essentially one-handed due to a stroke has special needs. Cutting meat or eating off a plate that is not stabilized is extremely difficult with one hand. We address these issues by inventing devices and utilizing adaptive devices. We care about function. In all the specialties, our job is to improve the quality of human life by improving the person's ability to function independently.

In the psychiatric or psychosocial setting, our objective is the same. We will use appropriate functional skills and activities to influence healthy ways to restore function that has been lost.

Occupational therapy is a diverse and comprehensive profession. OTs possess the scientific knowledge of how the physical body works in relation to daily activities and how to assess dysfunction or impairment in those areas. We also know how to evaluate and treat psychosocial function or dysfunction. In short, occupational therapy is an interesting mixed bag. OTs are professionals who may specialize in one area but whose goal is always to improve function on the function-to-dysfunction continuum and, therefore, improve the quality of life.

My expertise in OT includes primarily adult physical rehabilitation, hand therapy, psychiatric, geriatric, and cognitive rehabilitation.

Healing Practices

As a healer my practice involves what is commonly called energy field therapy or laying on of hands. This is not the same as the born-again or fundamentalist term "laying on of hands." Laying on of hands, as I practice it, does not have to do with one particular religion or personage. It is based on the system of energy that exists within all humans, that I have described as the human energy field or chakra system and the life force line or primary line of light.

Using this human energy field system to access information and communicate with people on deeper levels of consciousness

is part of what a healer does. Because the ability to do this healing work stems in a large part from being a practitioner of the
energetic spiritual disciplines of meditation, self-examination, and
prayer, healers are always developing their skills through their
application of these disciplines in their own lives and in their relationships to others. The healer, mystic, or shaman has a responsibility to his or her own soul's development and journey as well as
to every single soul the healer encounters. This concept of ever
expanding and practicing one's disciplines and skills can be
applied to any and every career, profession, or activity. In spiritual
healing work, it is of utmost importance to preserve the integrity
of the work itself and the spiritual principles to which healing
work is joined.

As a healer I have gained skills through meditation, self-
examination, and prayer that have provided me with many senses
that are sometimes referred to as clairvoyant, psychic, or mystical.
They are really natural to all who inhabit a human body. I, and
many others like myself, do spiritual disciplines regularly enough
to achieve regular mystical results. There are some exceptionally
gifted healers walking around in our country and every country
in the world.

Healing Stories

I am, and continue to be, a student of healing, and in this
capacity I am going to share some amazing healing stories with
you. The goal in sharing these stories is to demonstrate the healing ability all humans have and the spiritual destiny we all share.
Each and every soul in human form can attain an inner wisdom
in connection to a Higher Power. This inner wisdom heals and
allows for the miraculous to occur.

You may feel that some of these stories are more special, psychic, or miraculous than others. Indeed some may leap off the
page and strike your soul as significant and meaningful. That is as
it should be. I share them all with awe and wonder at the power
of the human spirit in its connection to the Divine. We are here

together, and it is our mission to assist one another in our journeys to ourselves and our Higher Power. With these things in mind I shall begin to weave the healing accounts I have witnessed and experienced.

Occupational Therapy and Healing

I was the director of occupational therapy at a teaching hospital in an inner-city area. As a matter of fact, I was in charge of developing the occupational therapy department for both inpatient care and outpatient services under the auspices of the rehabilitation department, which included the director of rehab who was a physical therapist, three staff physical therapists, a consultant part-time speech therapist, and myself. We worked with physiatrists, who are rehabilitation MDs, and, of course, all the referring physicians in the hospital whose patients required rehabilitation.

As a general practitioner OT with a special interest in hand therapy rehabilitation, I worked with many orthopedic surgeons and attending physicians in the hospital. I also have always loved psychosocial OT and therefore consulted in regular weekly hours with the department of psychiatry and ran weekly groups on the alcohol and drug detox unit as well as supervised the activities therapists on the inpatient psychiatric unit. My typical day involved treating outpatients in the rehab department in the morning, inpatients in the afternoon, and then psychiatry hours. I had been in the field of occupational therapy for four years prior to this particular job, working extensively in hospitals with the adult physical rehab population and in pediatrics in school settings.

The director of rehab was a fascinating fellow with a sense of humor that could be described as outrageous at times. For all his antics with the staff he was truly a marvelous physical therapist and healer. He was a consummate physical therapist with over twenty years of experience and possessed what I believe to be healing hands. He was a natural healer, though he claimed no healing practices other than his training as a physical therapist. He was well respected and universally liked for his affable and easygoing manner. His role as the director of rehab was important because his dedication to patient care was remarkable. He taught his students with the utmost care and shared his knowledge freely. In this department the healing journey blossomed for both patients and staff members. We all had our share of personal trials, tribulations, and character defects, but overall this juncture in the life cycle of those gathered was a place of professional and personal development.

It was under these circumstances that I began to consciously blend my healing work with my profession of occupational therapy. Now let us remember that many in the medical community do not believe in energy healing work, and if I said that life force energy could be channeled to come out of my hands and into my patient's scar tissue to break it up, I would be laughed at and mocked. I know this because I am part of the medical establishment. In addition if I told my co-workers that I had communicated spiritually or psychically with someone in a coma, they would probably think me a well-meaning sort who was a little screwy.

The tightrope I walked in openly discussing healing work was somewhat slippery. I knew I had to be an excellent OT who practiced within the guidelines of my licensed profession as well as being the healer I was becoming. Since most medical folks don't believe in or see auras, energy fields, or the actual energetic power of the mind and prayer, my co-workers didn't see anything wrong with what I said I was doing. I wasn't using any devices or treatments that weren't directly related to my OT work. If this "energy" I talked about wasn't seen, it wasn't real. I was just a quirky personality who otherwise did a very good job as an occupational therapist. However, as time unfolded I would become the one many of my co-workers would quietly come to when they were faced with uncomfortable or serious life situations and needed advice, comfort, or perhaps, as a last-ditch effort, a little of that spiritual energy work.

With my patients, I always went psychologically or spiritually where they were ready to go or where they were. I was simply their therapist and we developed our relationships together in the place where they were. If I felt a patient was open to spiritual or healing energy work I would explore this with him as an addition to the regular work we were doing together. I cannot recall one patient who did not wish to try this energy stuff.

The patients who come to a hospital rehab department are, for the most part, seriously injured or incapacitated in some way. For most, therapeutic intervention is a long process with small gains made weekly. When your life is so affected by an injury or disease process, you will often become willing to try something that previously may have sounded nutty to you; so it is with spiritual energy disciplines. Where we might have gotten along fine without them, all of a sudden the proverbial shit hits the fan and we are quite willing to try them. For all the patients who came into my life, I had but one desire: I wanted to best serve them and meet them where they were in a total way. For in a healer's belief system, every soul you encounter has a lesson to teach you about yourself and holds before you a mirror revealing who you are and a window to who they are.

His Decision
I was referred to the Intensive Care Unit (ICU) to see a comatose patient who I will call Mr. John. I was to assess his arms to see if he needed splints to prevent contractures and I was also to provide assisted movement to his arms and legs daily to maintain range of motion and prevent contractures.

I reviewed the medical chart prior to seeing the patient (standard protocol) to obtain all the relevant medical history and data. The patient, Mr. John, was a relatively young middle-aged man in the prime of his life—he had a career and a beautiful family—who had suffered a stroke that day and had lapsed into a coma. Mr. John was now on a respirator and technically considered near brain-dead. The damage to the brain was so extensive that no surgery or other intervention could reverse it. The prognosis was irreversible brain damage with resultant coma.

The only thing keeping this man alive was a respirator. My heart went out to his family who was devastated by his condition. My heart went out to Mr. John, too, who could no longer be with those he loved in the way he had every day up until now. And here I was, the OT who was supposed to go to his bedside and move his arms and legs for him so that he would not develop contractures. The ridiculousness of this struck me. This was not a machine lying before me, but a body with a human soul and consciousness attached to it until death.

I prayed before I walked into that room and asked Divine Spirit to guide me to serve this soul. I gently moved his arms and legs the way that I am trained to do, but as I did, I spoke with him both verbally and nonverbally. I introduced myself and explained how sorry I was that this had happened and how deeply I felt for his family and himself.

Suddenly the light above his bed flickered on and off. I realized he heard me with his soul/mind and we were communicating nonverbally. Mr. John was not able to open his eyes or communicate in any physical manner. The brain damage was too extensive. I was communicating with his spirit.

He wasn't quite sure of what had happened and so I explained his medical condition to him. I listened to him and felt his confusion. He needed time to understand and absorb what was going on. I finished doing my therapeutic exercises with him and told him I would visit him each day to do our exercises and be with him. The light above his bed again went on and off.

After I left, I stood outside his room as other staff went in and out and observed the light. Not once did it flicker in the manner it had when I was with him. It stayed constant. I kept my observation to myself and went about seeing my other patients and doing my work.

Mr. John and his family remained in my thoughts and prayers. Each day I would go to see him in ICU and do my OT duties while I spoke to him and listened to him. Always the light would respond at appropriate intervals to accentuate a communication.

After approximately a week in ICU, Mr. John was moved to another floor. He was medically in a persistent vegetative state in his coma and could live this way possibly for years depending on the continued capacity of his lungs and body to sustain physical life when artificially respirated. There was no way to tell when he would actually die because if his lungs and organs remained healthy he could be in this state for a long while. He would probably die of repeated bouts of pneumonia or other diseases that debilitate the body and eventually consume it, leaving the respirator with nothing left to respire.

Once Mr. John was moved to a medical floor in the hospital, the next step was to find a long-term care facility. Mr. John's death was not considered imminent at this point. I was now seeing Mr. John every afternoon and apprised him of this situation using our spirit/mind way of communicating. Mr. John let me know that he did not want to leave just yet. He was not reconciled to how his life had been disrupted by this medical condition. I joined him in his thoughts. I spoke to him about how terrible this must be for him and then spoke to him about his options. He could stay like this for a very long time, but what purpose did it serve? He couldn't be with his family or on the earth as he wanted to be, and so perhaps maybe it was time to move on. I spoke to him about the other side and those who were there waiting for him. Divine Spirit did indeed fill the room and the doorway between two worlds was open here. I told him that his was a difficult and painful situation, and that I would continue to pray for him. I gently held his hand and said that it was Friday and I would not be back again until Monday. A full three weeks had passed in our knowing each other. I said good-bye and left the hospital.

When I arrived at work on Monday, I learned that Mr. John had passed away within an hour of my leaving him. He had died with the respirator still breathing for him. His heart had stopped, and he had moved on.

Mr. John had made his decision. In that decision he had freed his family to mourn his death and move on with their lives. In that decision I saw a soul evolve in brilliance and courage to venture forth into the unknown. In that decision there was peace.

The Hand of Hope
The physiatrist (rehabilitation physician) called me into his office. Sitting there was a pretty young woman who looked very frightened, and had her right arm hidden beneath her coat. Standing

next to her was an older man who I eventually realized was her boyfriend. The physician asked the young woman to show me her right arm.

What I saw I had never seen before. The arm of this beautiful young woman was grotesquely deformed in the shape that is called "simian hand." The name is apt: the hand looks like an ape's hand rather than a human hand. It is severely clawed in appearance with the fingers curled up and the knuckles straightened and stretched tightly bending backward (not forward as in a fist). In addition the wrist is positioned in extreme flexion, giving a limp-wristed appearance, and contracted, which means that all the muscles and tendons on the inside of the arm are shortened and one is unable to pull the wrist out of this position.

There were multiple contractures throughout the wrist, hand, and fingers owing to an injury this young woman had sustained. She had been attacked with an ax by her ex-boyfriend. To complicate the rehabilitation effort further, the injury and surgical repair had occurred over eight months before the young woman first appeared for rehab.

The physician explained to the young woman that she would need to come to see me for therapy three times weekly to treat her arm and we might possibly be able to improve its appearance. We scheduled an appointment and she and her boyfriend left.

The physician then came into my office and threw his arms into the air. "There is not much we can do here," he said. "It is over eight months old and we are not even sure the nerves are intact." What this meant was that this young woman was unable to move her wrist or hand at all and it was permanently stuck in this grotesque posture. The patient had been referred to us by the hand clinic's orthopedic surgeon. I called him and spoke with him about the case. His reaction was as exasperated as the physiatrist's. "Don't expect much improvement; the damage is old now." He had not done the surgery and was not sure that the tendons, muscles, and nerves were viable or properly repaired. There was so much scar tissue at the site of injury (midforearm on the inside of the arm) that assessing tendon or muscle glide was nearly impossible and, as there was no clinical evidence of nerve regeneration at this point, the prognosis was gloomy. I had an extremely challenging case. What now follows is a summary of a course of treatment that lasted over ten months.

The patient, who I shall call Ms. Hope, was scheduled for an electromyography (EMG) eleven days after her initial visit for therapy with me. An EMG is a test whereby nerve damage or nerve function can be assessed by placing a small needle connected to amplifiers and recorders into a muscle belly to monitor the electrical activity of the motor units or nerves of the muscle. Due to the fact that there were no clinical signs of regeneration of the severed nerves (ulnar and median) in the eight months since the ax attack and subsequent surgery, the possibility of good peripheral nerve regeneration was at this point grim.

"A completely severed peripheral nerve has some capacity to repair itself. The growth rate is approximately 1 to 2 millimeters per day. *Chance* apparently determines whether a regenerating motor fiber (nerve fiber) enters a neurilemmal tube leading to a motor or sensory terminal. If suitably matched, connections with a motor end plate (that which stimulates the muscle) can be re-established and function restored. Nerve fibers of the brain and spinal cord, however, do not regenerate effectively."[1]

To make this important technical explanation clear: a completely cut nerve in the arm or leg has some ability to repair itself. If the repair does occur, it normally happens at a rate of one to two millimeters a day. However, it appears that *chance* determines this repair. It may happen and it may not. There is no sure bet. It's all up to *chance*.

In Ms. Hope's case, eight months had elapsed with no movement or sensation below the level of injury to demonstrate nerve regeneration. *Chance* had apparently not occurred as of yet; the new nerve growth that could have occurred by the time of our first visit might have been as much as 48 centimeters, which would have demonstrated itself in clinical assessment for movement

---

[1]Excerpted from *Manter and Gatz's Essentials of Clinical Neuroanatomy and Neurophysiology*, Edition 7 "Regeneration of Nerve Fiber," Philadelphia: F. A. Davis, 1987, p. 70.

and sensation in the hand. This means she could have had noticeable/measureable movement of her fingers at this point. This was not the case as the EMG demonstrated.

During our four visits prior to the EMG, Ms. Hope and I had already reviewed the standard treatment options—manual stretching, scar tissue massage, heat (fluidoltherapy), splinting (devices designed to reposition and gradually stretch the wrist, forearm, and hand back toward a more normal position) and an alternative treatment of energy therapy. Ms. Hope listened as I explained the energy field concept and how I could actually try to run life force energy into her nerves and muscles simply by using my hands. Ms. Hope clearly stated that she had nothing to lose and would try it. We began the arduous and painful therapy sessions that involved all of the above standard therapy techniques and the additional energy field techniques.

Eleven days after our initial visit the EMG findings revealed extensive damage to two of the three nerves in the right arm at the site of injury extending to the hand with nerve root shrinkage and possible signs of new nerve life. Now, medically speaking, if nerve growth had been occurring for the last eight months, there would be much greater nerve function and motor function (movement) returning to this young woman's arm. She had had disruption and total loss of motor, sensory, and sympathetic (perspiring) function of her ulnar and median nerves. Even good surgical repair of the nerves under excellent conditions results in limited functional recovery. Ms. Hope's hand showed all the signs of the most severe type of nerve damage after eight months. It is easy to see why the doctors had told me not to expect much. There really wasn't much medical hope of recovery in this hand.

However, there was a lot of hope for Ms. Hope. Although she came in for her appointments erratically and chronically late, we were developing a relationship and I was getting to know her as a person. Our backgrounds were very different. Ms. Hope had not finished high school and was living with a man much older than herself. She was afraid to leave her house because of what had happened and what she now looked like. She always hid the grotesque hand beneath a coat.

As time went on we addressed many issues other than Ms. Hope's hand. I confronted Ms. Hope regarding her absences and her chronic lateness and told her I would no longer treat her if she would not keep her appointments. Ms. Hope attended regularly thereafter and always came on time. We became friends. She no longer hid her hand, which was splinted and becoming more normal looking. At each appointment Ms. Hope would ask for the energy treatment. She said she could feel the energy when I performed it, and that this was more important to her than the other therapy work.

We were seeing amazing results. She was getting movement of her wrist, forearm, and fingers. Ms. Hope was able to use her right hand for activities she thought she would never be able to do again. The day she could put curlers in her hair using both her hands was a day of celebration. She was seeing results, and all the tears spilled during the painful stretching and merciless scar tissue massage were becoming tears of joy.

When I saw the small muscles inside her hand working and moving her fingers up and down and side to side, it was a clear clinical sign that nerve regeneration was occurring to the most intricate muscles of her fingers and to the muscles that are moved by the two nerves that had been severed. (The third nerve, the radial nerve, had been uninvolved; however, it supplies or moves different muscle groups than the ulnar/median nerves.) The *chance* of regeneration of her nerves coincided with her initiation of occupational therapy and alternative energy field therapy. That this chance had not occurred in the eight months prior is a mystery.

The hand surgeon, upon seeing Ms. Hope's recovery stated that it was indeed miraculous and that he should have taken pictures so that he could present this amazing case. There was still further to go in the rehabilitation of the hand, and the sensory loss was still apparent. Sensation is a far more difficult nerve function to restore once lost. However, such significant gains were made that the entire rehab team was impressed.

The physicians who had thrown their hands in the air and told me not to expect too much were clearly baffled. This was a case for the books. But Ms. Hope and I weren't baffled. We knew that with only standard treatment there would not have been such a quick and miraculous recovery. "That energy thing," as Ms. Hope called it, was the primary recovery factor in the *chance* occurrence of nerve regeneration. No one can sway me or Ms. Hope to believe otherwise. We were there together and we saw the miracle of love and energy and plain old-fashioned hard work pay off.

(I would love to be involved in medical research that would investigate this claim of possible nerve regeneration facilitated by energy field therapy. Perhaps now or in the near future medical professionals will receive funding for such research.)

Ready for Motherhood

Belinda was the most soft-spoken and shy woman I had ever worked with and she was by far the sweetest physical therapist on staff at the hospital. She never had a bad word to say about anyone or anything. When all the staff enjoyed needling me about my spiritual healing work and would call me the Dali Llama (with affection of course), she would quietly smile and tell me she knew I was sincere. A sweetheart of a co-worker, she had been married for ten years to a kind man who was also a physical therapist.

Belinda came into my office one day with a request. She was slightly uncomfortable when she sat down to talk. She explained to me that her husband and she had been earnestly trying to have a baby for over a year. Her doctor had told her that he wanted to proceed to fertility drugs since she was now considered clinically infertile. She said that she knew about my spiritual energy work and asked if there was something I could possibly do to help her. I said of course I would try.

That day we met in the treatment room on our lunch hour. Before going there, though, I prayed and meditated as I do before working with any patient. Assisting someone in becoming pregnant is a solemn responsibility. When you are doing deep spiritual work the burden of interfering or assisting with divine plan is upon you. I, for one, always try to stay within the realm of working with divine plan and err on the side of caution against manipulating energy to suit my desires, no matter how well-intentioned they may be.

Remember, too, I was feeling my way in this work and was quite concerned about the actual power I was witnessing and its effects on others and myself. All was directed toward helping another, yet healers need be ever vigilant for the ego or the small-minded self will that always pops up.

I prayed very hard and meditated very hard. Once transported through prayer and meditation to a calm and serenely guided state of mind, I went to work on Belinda. It became quite clear that she would be the most wonderful mother and she just needed an adjustment on the polarization (energetic charge) of her ovaries (a technique taught by the Reverend Rosalyn Bruyere) and an overall charging of her life force and chakra system. I did this, and then was succinctly informed that Belinda would become pregnant within the next month and that if her baby was a girl, she would name her Sarah.

I hesitated to tell Belinda what I had been told. How could I tell her she would get pregnant next month if it then did not happen? This was a dire responsibility for me. However, I was learning to discern clear guidance from unclear guidance and trusted infinitely in Divine Wisdom and the love I felt present during the healing session. I told Belinda that she would become pregnant within the next month. I asked her if it was a girl what she would name her, and she smiled sweetly and replied, "Sarah." I knew I had done the right thing in telling her.

Belinda did indeed become pregnant the very next month and has since given birth to a beautiful, healthy baby boy. Divine Spirit didn't say the child would be a girl, just what Belinda would have named her if she was a girl. As a matter of further information, a boy's name had not been chosen at the time of the healing. Spirit is very wise.

The Atheist

Paul was a physical therapist who worked with me in a local nursing home. He was a self-admitted atheist who did not believe in psychic healing, spiritual healing, or human energy fields but did very strongly believe in the almighty dollar. He was a very industrious businessman in addition to being a physical therapist, and he had a marvelous gift for conversation and igniting passionate discussions about subjects he did not believe in. Both of Paul's parents were in the medical field and since his youth he had been versed in the language of medicine.

Paul came into my office one day unable to move his neck. He had undergone physical therapy treatments of massage, ultrasound, and electric stimulation all to no avail. He had, as well, received cortisone injections in an attempt to relieve the pain and return motion to his neck. Nothing had worked, and so he asked me if I could work on him to relieve his pain. He was desperate and in obvious discomfort.

I asked him to come lie down on the therapy mat and I initiated the energy field therapy. I worked on Paul's energy field for approximately thirty minutes. Because I am an OT, I often combine energy field work with physical touch or mobilization techniques. However, in this particular case I felt that laying on of hands would be most appropriate without great physical manipulation.

I started my energy work first by scanning his entire energy field with my hands and spiritual vision and then went to work at his feet. He seemed perturbed by this and told me the problem was in his neck not his feet. I told him to be quiet if he wanted me to treat him, that I would get to his neck eventually. (This was in keeping with our relationship.) I did indeed work my way up to his neck and head and when we were done he got up and moved his neck fully with absolutely no pain. He looked incredulous and continued to move his neck back and forth. "You're a witch," he accused, still moving his neck back and forth. I laughed at him and told him I'd been called worse.

Recovered somewhat from his shock, he asked me why this energy field therapy had worked when he did not believe in it. Very good question. I explained to him that if an appendix is ruptured, a surgeon can remove the offending appendix from the patient even if the patient does not believe in surgery. Surely he himself must have some patients who do not believe in physical therapy but do get results from the treatments. He agreed. We went on to discuss how some patients will get better faster when they are convinced of the efficacy of a therapy, and others will not recover from the same injury because they do not believe they can recover. It was a complicated metaphysical and psychological discussion.

Certainly not everyone will achieve the same healing benefits from any medical or alternative therapy, but that does not
mean that the therapies are ineffective for all or that one has to
believe in them for them to work. Higher consciousness has a lot
more information on that score and possibly there was a larger
reason for pain-free neck motion to return to the man who doth
protest too much. I will tell you that Paul no longer hurled vexing or denigrating remarks my way regarding the energy field
work I did. The results had spoken for themselves. Paul still
claims to be an atheist. Spiritual energy does not discriminate
against nonbelievers; it is an equal opportunity employer.

My Irascible Friend

At one of the nursing homes I had a patient I will call Mr. Irascible.
I have so named him because of the ire he would arouse in any and
every person who came in contact with him. Mr. Irascible was confined to a wheelchair (as are many nursing home residents) and was
very angry about his debilitating condition. He would cuss and yell
at everyone and then laugh heartily at the turmoil he caused.

Mr. Irascible was referred for occupational therapy by his
attending physician because his physical condition was deterio-
rating and his doctor thought that possibly OT could restore some
of Mr. Irascible's lost function. What was happening was that Mr.
Irascible was not able to propel his wheelchair well anymore. His
legs did not work at all though they had just months before. Even
his arms were growing weaker and his endurance was diminish-
ing. It was documented on his medical record that he had sustained possible transient ischemic attacks (mini-strokes) and a
CVA (cerebral vascular accident) or stroke prior to this current
debilitation and that possibly this was now recurring.

Mr. Irascible showed up at my therapy door each morning
complaining, "My legs don't work anymore." Mr. Irascible was
angry that physical therapy wasn't working because he still
couldn't walk and was getting worse. He cared very much about
the loss of his legs for standing and walking and wasn't as concerned about the arm exercises and wheelchair exercises I was
going to give him. But he showed up at the therapy door every
single day and we proceeded with treatment. To appease Mr.

Irascible I would put him in the standing table to do some arm exercises and activities while standing. Of course he was being held in a standing position by a box which totally supported his weight when he leaned his butt against the wooden support behind him.

We became friendly as time went on and he heard mention of something special I could do that he called the "hoodoo voodoo." Mr. Irascible insisted that I try this energy work on him because he felt nothing else was working. I felt, of course, deep compassion for his pain and frustration, enough to overcome my fear that the nursing home could throw me out on my ear for practicing "hoodoo voodoo" on Mr. Irascible. I began doing energy field therapy with Mr. Irascible in conjunction with his standard OT treatment plan. Mr. Irascible reported feeling increased physical comfort and demonstrated an increasingly friendly tone with all those in the OT room.

His physical condition was truthfully not showing much sign of improvement and had remained medically unexplained as no new evidence of strokes or CIAs was evinced through diagnostic tests. I decided to enter the energy field to see what the exact nature of the problem was. "Entering" the energy field means that I was attempting to use my own energy field and consciousness in a meditative and prayerful state to find the reason for Mr. Irascible's illness. I traversed his body using my clairvoyant vision and senses and entered into what is known as the cerebral spinal fluid where I saw swimming organisms that looked to me like sperm. I was told very clearly by my guidance that Mr. Irascible had neurosyphilis. I was astounded and dismayed. We finished our work together and I did not mention this information to this patient. First, I am not a physician, and second, I wasn't sure of what to do with this information.

I went home that night and spoke with my husband who happens to be a physician and asked him what organism in the cerebral spinal fluid looks like a sperm. After I told my husband the story, he informed me it was possibly a spirochete and if in the cerebral spinal fluid could be an indication of tertiary or neurosyphilis. I explained my dilemma. How could I possibly find out if this indeed was the case? My husband explained that I could approach the attending physician and ask him to do a special test called an FTA/ABS, which would diagnose tertiary syphilis. Apparently at the tertiary stage of syphilis the test commonly known as a VDRL will turn up a false negative result, but the FTA/ABS will be accurate.

The very next day I saw the attending physician on one of the resident floors doing chartwork. I said hello and began to speak with him about the patient in question. I told him that Mr. Irascible may be manifesting the later stages of syphilis and asked if maybe we could run an FTA/ABS to determine if this was the case. He flew into an angry tirade. "My patient does not have syphilis; I have been treating him for over seven years and I know this is not the case." He turned away from me. Still I persisted. "You know, since we really don't know medically what is causing this deterioration of function in Mr. Irascible, don't you think we could, for teaching reasons, run this simple blood test to rule out this diagnosis?" The physician looked quizzically at me and a listening nurse chimed in "You know doctor, it could just be a routine test; it wouldn't harm anything."

The physician consented and ordered bloodwork. The test came back with what is called a positive reactive 3. The physician did not believe the results and ordered a second test. Again the results came back positive reactive 3, clearly indicating the patient did have tertiary syphilis. When I saw the physician he threw the results at me. "Since when does an OT become a diagnostician?" The physician was very annoyed with me. I decided to explain to him that I saw the spirochetes in the patient's cerebral spinal fluid and had been told that this was the problem through spiritual guidance.

Instead of laughing at me, he was intrigued. He asked if I could possibly treat a difficult case of idiopathic hypertension that was not responding to any hypertensive drugs I said I could try, and he appeared delighted. He then informed me that if I could reduce this particular patient's blood pressure he would be impressed because he had closely monitored this patient over a long course of time and actually took the patient's blood pressure daily at different times and under many circumstances. He knew that nothing thus far had regulated the patient's blood pressure— hence the name idiopathic hypertension.

"Nothing like a little pressure and medical scrutiny under which to perform energy field therapy," I thought, but I complied with his request and met the patient outside of the nursing home at a private location. The physician was present and monitored the patient's blood pressure prior to my work. When I had completed my work, the patient's blood pressure was again measured. Astonishingly, it was, for the first time in a long while, within a safe range. It was significantly lower than in the initial measurement—a largely significant difference.

I informed the physician that unless the patient changed his lifestyle, his blood pressure would not become regulated. The energy work had revealed a deeply angry and bitter man. Nothing would work unless the patient worked on himself and his whole attitude toward his life and himself. I do not think this information counted for much. I was asked back again and this time I was unable to achieve the same results. The patient was very resistive to the energy work and the suggestions that he change his life and attitudes. I was never asked back again, and this physician and I never really had much more direct interaction.

Mr. Irascible's condition was explained to him by his physician. Mr. Irascible would not accept the diagnosis and continued to fight on for the return of his lost function. At the end stages of tertiary syphilis there is no antibiotic nor drug therapy that will help. The disease is too far advanced. For many reasons that are deeply spiritual and private for Mr. Irascible, I knew that all I could do energetically and spiritually was to make Mr. Irascible as physically comfortable as possible and continue to support him in his quest for greater independent function. There would be no physical cure here, but a spiritual journey was unfolding within Mr. Irascible's life.

Not all physical disease can be cured. Nor is it my job or anyone else's to assume to know the divine workings of Spirit in another's life. We can be fully present and show up for Divine Spirit to manifest itself, but only Divine Spirit knows what is and must be. I will continue to my best ability to show up daily. There are miracles of Spirit that are greater than physical disease.

The Meditation and Healing Group

I was now leading a meditation and healing group weekly in the evening. Attendance varied, but there was a core of approximately seven individuals who attended regularly. All the participants were interested in energy field therapy, and some were beginners in practicing healing or alternative therapy in the human energy field area as well as other alternative therapy practices.

My goal was to facilitate meditative states and healing work and we used all the spiritual energy practices each week. A distinct love and honesty permeated the dwelling place when the spiritual disciplines were initiated. A proliferation of powerful healing events was generated for all members and for many others brought there as well.

The group itself was composed of many successful and interesting people from varied professions and backgrounds. There were only a few individuals in the medical profession. This is important to note here, for much wonderful healing work and psychotherapeutic spiritual work was done in this group simply by practicing the spiritual energy disciplines. Physical healing was not the sole purpose here. The group included a mixture of all religious backgrounds, but we were joined together in this spiritual work where all thought systems were included and none excluded. All the participants desired to increase their abilities to meditate, pray, self-examine, and to acquire the more clairvoyant or extrasensory awareness that would connect them consciously to the stream of universal consciousness and to their Higher Power. These gifts and abilities did occur for all those present. There was a conscious evolving in spiritual purpose for all of the participants. Personalities and differences aside, all the members experienced a powerful spiritual presence and the awakenings of personal healing journeys. I will relate to you some of the extraordinary healing stories that occurred in this group.

A New Liver

One evening when our meditation group met, one of the members told us about a devastating and life-threatening illness that had overcome a longtime friend. The individual who was ill was a twenty-three-year-old woman who had had an acute onset of fulminant hepatic failure of unknown etiology. Translation: her liver had stopped functioning for unknown reasons and she was being transported to a regional transplant center that evening for a potential liver transplant operation the next day. This was an extremely urgent situation, and the only hope for cure was a liver transplant.

Because all human energy fields and the mind and consciousness are energetically joined, one can do spiritual healing work on a person who is not physically present. The human energy field contains the blueprint for the physical body and is connected to the physical body. What is done is to actually bring all the spiritual consciousness in the gathered healing circle to the consciousness of the human energy field or soul that requires assistance. We, as a group, actually brought the consciousness of this young woman's human energy field to our group.

We entered into a deeply prayerful and meditative state, all joined in one purpose, to assist this young woman to health. In the hands of the Higher Power, we went to work. We actually felt, saw, and worked on restoring health to her liver by having her liver in the collective minds and consciousness of the group and by directing the healing first chakra red energy to her liver, which desperately needed it. We prayed and sent energy and guided healing energy to the liver. We bathed it in healing energetic vibration to cleanse and restore life force energy to it and to the young woman's entire energy system. We were, of course, joined with and in surrender to our Higher Power's divine guidance and wisdom. We ended this healing session when we felt the work was done, and we moved on to other meditations and healing work.

The group member who had brought the story of this young woman to our group found out later the following day that during the previous night the young woman's liver was returned to normal functioning with no need for surgery. The doctors were baffled and said it was miraculous that the liver had so quickly returned to healthy functioning. There was no obvious medical reason why. Our group, of course, needed no medical explanations. We had witnessed the miracle of healing through prayer and joined energy therapy. The doorway between spirit and physical life was open, and we had worked in conjunction with a presence greater than ourselves and were grateful that Divine Spirit had worked this miracle. Thy will be done; we had just showed up and tried.

A Troubled Soul

On another evening of the meditation and healing group, one of our members came in with a request for a healing on a young woman whom he had known since childhood and had recently spoken to, although he had not seen her for years. He told her that he was involved in a spiritual healing group and that his path in life was now a spiritual one. She shared with him that she was HIV positive, had AIDS, and was very ill. Her lifestyle was not a healthy one, and she was not attempting to change it. He counseled her on better nutrition and seeking good health care to improve her wellness while living with HIV. She had not embraced these suggestions, but she did ask him if maybe the group he belonged to might work on her sometime. He said he would ask the group to do so.

Upon his request, the group decided to try to help. Once again we entered a prayerful and meditative state and energetically brought the group to this girl's human energy field or her human energy field to the group (whichever way you choose to view it). Time and distance do not exist in spiritual realms as they do in earth planes, but all are joined.

I saw clearly before us the girl we were to work on and positioned all the members around her energy field so that we could each send healing life force energy into her chakra system and primary line of light system. She was extremely thin, and frail with dark hair and eyes. (I had not seen her before, nor had she been physically described to us.) We all began to direct healing energy as guided. Because I was the leader, I guided the healing effort. As I looked upon her energy system, I noted that the seat of her soul (the place the soul sits in the body with outstretched wings across the chest) was blackened in one place. The soul normally possesses a gold-white and shining radiance. Looking closer, I realized this was not her true soul, but the disease had become a part of her soul. As a healer I knew that it did not belong in her soul just as cancer does not belong in a body, and I attempted to remove it. It was a difficult task and the blackened place was difficult to remove. I did the best I could, and we continued our prayer and energy work and then gently finished.

The next day our group member received a call from the young girl we had worked on. She explained to him that she had gone to bed early that evening and had had the strangest dream. A young woman with long dark hair had tried to steal a part of her soul. He explained to her that the group had worked on her as she had requested and that some of the healing work was done on the soul level. He had never described any group members to this young woman. I had long dark hair at the time of that healing, and I am sure that what I was doing energetically felt to this young woman like I was stealing a part of her soul. That it was black and did not belong there did not matter. It had become part of what she felt was her soul.

Since the young woman had requested a healing we had obliged. Healing work does not always feel perfectly comfortable as any medical, psychotherapeutic, or spiritual practice does not. The goal, of course, is increased comfort and peace but the process can feel uncomfortable at times.

I do not desire to invade someone's soul or take a part she does not wish to give up. That is not what I as a healer will do. I could only attempt, at a request, to do that which I am trained to do: bring healing life force and remove destructive energy to allow for healing. In any and every case the soul who owns the energy field makes its own decisions regarding the disposition of a healing that is first surrendered to Divine Wisdom. I knew in my heart that I had only tried to assist this young woman toward health and I must own the responsibility of my actions. And I do.

There is an immense responsibility associated with healing work and unless you feel ready to be responsible for touching other souls, do not do so. But we always touch other souls in everyday living and can be sure that if we stay aligned with our own spiritual practices we will do so with increasing love and clarity that are the gifts of spiritual energy practices. Not everyone is meant to be an alternative energy healer like myself just as all do not choose the same professions or jobs. But we all can learn to become connected to our own soul's journey and a higher wisdom which directs our lives to joy.

It is important for me to note here that not all physical illness becomes lodged in the soul in blackness. This was an end-stage result of many factors, only one of which was the HIV infection. As a matter of fact, there are many glistening white and gold luminescent souls that have bodies living healthfully and with HIV. Those glistening souls walk a path of beauty and powerful healing for others to see. Having an illness or virus does not mean that our souls are tarnished or shrouded. Quite the contrary, many times our illnesses serve to give birth to soul illumination and emanation. Let us always remain with open hearts and open eyes. Our young woman friend passed away within the next year. God rest and God bless.

Through regular practice of meditation, self-examination, and prayer all of the group members were brought to new levels of spiritual awareness and connection to their life's journey joined to Divine Spirit. All who came and went from the group felt that there had been a power of special spiritual energy in our weekly group that had deeply affected their lives. Collectively, our group had been a stepping-stone on the evolving life path that each of us would take. As life is an ever changing and moving event, so was our group. We all eventually moved on to other places for our growth. It had been a miraculous journey at a certain time.

Healing in Daily Life

I continue my work as a healer and occupational therapist. Healing work is not a separate part or compartment of one's life.

It is one's life and, as such, my personal life is as full of healing stories and practices as is my professional life. Our spiritual practices become our way of life, and all of life is experienced from this perspective. Thank goodness I have a life partner at this time who understands whom he is living with and is devoted to living from a spiritual perspective. He is also a medical doctor and very grounded in the realities of the world, a perfect partner for one who prefers to live on celestial realms. He always has a way to pull me back into my feet. He also has a wonderful way of poking fun and joking about much of this work when I get too serious.

On the Road Again

Due to the busy and responsible nature of our work my husband and I relish our vacations. They are restorative and give us a chance to explore the world. On one such badly-needed vacation we set out by car to travel south of New York City. At the time, my husband was a medical resident. His hours were long, the pay was poor, and he was often exhausted. We never saw enough of each other, so our vacations were our time to be entirely alone with one another. The hours driving in the car were special hours to talk and renew our knowing each other. We were excited to be traveling to locations we hadn't been to before and, with work miles away and long forgotten, we arrived at our first rest stop for dinner and a hotel night's sleep.

After checking into our room, we showered and prepared for dinner. We asked the hotel clerk which nearby restaurant he might recommend and compared his suggestions to those in our book of recommended lodgings and restaurants. We settled on a nearby steak house and took a leisurely walk to our much-anticipated first evening's dinner. We arrived at our destination and were seated at our table. The hostess handed us our menus, and we eagerly opened them to decide on our dinner fare. A waitress came to our table with glasses of water and prepared to take our order. As yet undecided, we ordered an appetizer and beverages.

When the waitress left, I spoke to my husband.

"She is very angry and upset and I am supposed to help her."

My husband looked at me and said, "Oh no, you're not going to start this on our vacation with a complete stranger."

I looked at him and shrugged. "I have to try and help her. They are telling me to."

My husband knew it was inevitable, for when Spirit beckoned, I had learned to listen. The waitress returned with our drinks and asked to take our order.

"I hope you don't think I am crazy," I began, "but I have a feeling that you are very upset or angry about something and—"

The waitress cut me off. "I am not upset about anything," she spoke curtly between closed lips.

"Oh well, I just thought that perhaps I might be able to help you with your problem and—"

Again she cut me off. "I don't have a problem, okay?" She smiled thinly and asked about our order.

We ordered our food, and my husband looked over at me. "Are you finished now? She doesn't want your help."

"I have to try and help her. I know it seems crazy, but I'm being very powerfully nudged."

Our waitress returned with our appetizer and a basket of bread. I decided to try a different angle.

"I'm sorry if I upset you, it's just that I'm a spiritual healer, and I was informed that I may be able to help you."

The waitress looked intensely at me. "Oh yeah, well how the hell are you going to help me? You want to know what my problem is? I'll tell you. I am thirty-nine years old and have finally met and married the man I truly love only to find out I can't get pregnant. I have been on fertility drugs and been through all sorts of tests as has my husband, and we cannot have a baby. How in the world are you going to help me?" She stared angrily at me.

"Well there is a technique I have learned that I think will help. It is part of energy healing work, and I believe that if I am allowed to work on you with this healing energy I can help you in your quest for a baby."

She looked at me, then my husband. My husband adjoined, "Look, I know this may sound unusual, but I am a physician and my wife is in the medical field. She's not crazy; she really can do this spiritual healing work and although I do not fully understand it, she has had amazing results."

With this, the waitress said she would be right back. When she came out of the kitchen she again approached our table.

"I just spoke to my husband who happens to own the restaurant. I don't believe in this stuff at all, but he says we have tried everything else, so what harm could this do? How do we do it?" She was waiting for a reply.

"Well I don't need any special circumstances, but it would be nice for us to be in a more quiet, private space for us to work and where you could sit down," I replied.

We settled on the backyard of the restaurant, which had a pretty garden and a bench where we could sit. We decided to do the healing work after we had dinner. As dinner went on we inquired further about her medical history. She was not currently taking fertility drugs and had stopped for quite some time to rest her body.

We finished our meal and coffee and went out back.

My husband was present but hers was not. I asked her to sit upon the bench and after entering a prayerful and meditative state went to work on her energy field.

This was a woman with a deep yearning to parent and share her love with a child. She had been through so very many difficult experiences that this last frustration was surely enough to evoke deep resentment. A healer learns much more than one would normally reveal to others. We go deeply into the soul energy field we are touching and must do so in profound honor and with compassion for the trials and beauty of those souls we touch.

She remarked how peaceful she now felt. I went on with the work and realized it was slightly more involved than simply repolarization of the ovaries. I did the necessary work entirely guided by Spirit. At the close of the session I was told by guidance that she would get pregnant in the following month and give birth to a girl. Of course I hesitated to tell her this, ethically and morally. This woman had been through so much. Again, with the burden of being responsible and yet trusting the Divine Guidance I had learned to listen to, I went forward.

"My guidance tells me you will get pregnant next month and you will have a little girl." She smiled genuinely and said she hoped it was true. We hugged (I hugged her actually) and my husband and I departed. She had been given our address and phone number to keep in touch if she so chose. My husband and I continued our road trip.

Weeks and then months passed and still I had not heard from our waitress. Each time I sat to meditate on the situation I was told she was indeed pregnant and would have a little girl. As time progressed, my rational mind told me that if it had worked I would have heard from her with the joyous news. Still I did not hear and yet Spirit always assured me that she was pregnant with a girl.

Six months after our encounter, I received a card in the mail. It was from our waitress. It stated that she was indeed pregnant and it happened exactly as I had said it would. She had conceived the month following the healing and was having a little girl. The note further went on to state that this course of events would always remain a mystery to her. She questioned if I had really anything to do with it. She thanked me though, for my spirit.

I wrote to her. I told her how happy I was for her. I also told her that the Higher Power has no ego that requires massage, only humans do, and that maybe in time her mystery would further reveal itself to her.

This experience certainly had an effect on my humanness. If she had gone to the doctor and was told exactly when she would conceive and what the sex of her child would be as a result of the procedure and these events had unfolded exactly as the doctor had said, I wondered if it would have been a mystery to her. This, though, is the dilemma of all humankind at times. We do not recognize the gifts Spirit brings nor openly acknowledge that truly it is of that we call Spirit. I hope her mystery will become clear in time, and that healers will continue to show up and do their work trusting only the truth of whom they serve.

One Bright Shining Star

There are those with whom I have shared close relationships and observed the fruits of their practices of the spiritual energy disciplines. Although not healers by profession, they were healers within their own lives and demonstrated the miracles of love and life from a divinely awakened inner place. One such glorious soul walked in my life for too brief a physical earth time. His is a story of joy and gladness although it sprang from a fountain of immense sadness.

When I met Peter he was a rough and jaded character. We both belonged to a fellowship that teaches spirituality and soul evolvement through twelve divine steps. We went to fellowship meetings together and learned of the twelve step way of life and our paths separated. I went on my life's journey exploring this newfound twelve step spirituality. Peter followed his path as well. Five years later we met again through a mutual friend. I found out that Peter was gravely ill with AIDS and yet, to my happiness, he had been living a clean and sober life for the past two years.

I drove out to meet Peter where he was living, and we saw each other for the first time in many years. Peter was very ill. He could only walk with great difficulty as his balance had been affected by the ravages of AIDS-related illnesses. We spoke of the past five years and the changes that had occurred in both our lives.

At this point I was very seriously involved in metaphysical studies and was learning meditation and developing my relationship to God on more fervent and expanding levels. I was not yet a conscious practitioner of energy healing but knew that the only way to happiness and miracles was through the peace of God.

I asked Peter about his relationship to God. He looked at me softly and said he did not yet have one. But he now dearly desired such a relationship. And so we traveled together to spiritual workshops and healing circles that espoused the spirituality of inner exploration, meditation, and prayer.

Peter found his way. In our coming together with the mission of finding God, we accomplished our work together. More than anything, Peter discovered that he desperately desired to find and marry his soul mate. It was not to be me, for that was neither the goal nor the fruit of our relationship, which was a friendship. Although I deeply loved Peter and wished that he would be able to fulfill this deep longing, my rational mind wanted to tell him that his soul's desire for a marriage and mate would not necessarily become a physical reality, but this would not mean that his requests to God had been unanswered.

Peter persisted in all areas to develop his connection to a Higher Power and his own soul. He directed his energy toward starting a support group for people living with AIDS and continued diligently on the path of meditation, self-examination, and prayer. His life had deep purpose and meaning, and he was busy from dawn to dusk doing his work in the world and in himself.

During one afternoon's conversation early in our reacquaintance, Peter had asked me to promise to write his story someday. I had responded at the time that his story was not yet completed and that he could write it himself in time. He grabbed my hand and made me promise. I told him I would when the time came. Little did I know that my initial response was to be so prophetic.

Peter's story had just begun. He went on to meet a beautiful, vivacious, and loving young woman who shared his vision and life. They were married and continued their work together helping and healing others through their miraculous love and their work with support groups. The last time I spoke with Peter he told me how happy he was. His dream had come true. When he physically passed from this earth to the next realm, he did so having accomplished his deepest desire. Peter's life had become a miracle unfolding in all directions when he embraced his true self and God. Peter's life still touches those who knew of him and those who know him still.

True healing in each life is coming to know the inner connected divine self and doing that which brings one's deepest spiritual desires to reality. We cannot always see or anticipate the outcome of our heartfelt desires, but we can strive to fulfill our yearnings in our spiritual practices. Faith, trust, and true love walk hand in hand with those who learn to listen to their hearts and souls. Courageous are they who follow their dreams, despite the doubts of the rational-minded majority that surrounds them. For there is a Greater Mind that works miracles for those who follow their soul's true path. Let us all learn courage.

Chapter 8

※

HEALING THE SELF WITH ENERGY

The healing stories shared with the reader in the previous chapter simply describe experiences in which self-examination, meditation, and prayer were used to energetically augment healing. Whether the impact of that healing was felt most greatly in the mind, the heart, the soul, or the body varied with each individual. In each case, healing encompasses all of these areas. The link between the healings is that they were done through the use of life force energy. Since the world we live in, our physical bodies, our minds, and our souls are all energetically alive life force systems, we can direct healing energy within the body, mind, spirit continuum by using spiritual energetic exercises and principles. Such practices affect all that we are as human beings.

Just as not all of us are going to be physicians, psychotherapists, or clergy, not all of us are going to become professional or community healers. But what we all can become are aware and responsible self-healers. Any good physician will tell you that the patient knows her own body better than the physician does. The same is true of the self-examination or psychotherapeutic process. We can be guided and enlightened by another in the process of self-examination, but the work, change, and self-awareness must be our own. The same is true of our spirituality. There are those whose lives are devoted to a religious course and they can give guidance, but the relationship between oneself and Spirit is between oneself and Spirit. Each of us ultimately is left within our own body, mind, and spirit: only you are best suited to hear, feel, know, and relate to all that you are. Through self-awareness and self-knowing, we can help ourselves in an energetic and spiritual context.

There are spontaneous healings, miracles, and unexplained recoveries from illness. Science does not have all the answers, nor does any human being. The most effective way to experience miracles and self-healing is to practice those spiritual activities that bring you into the realm of healing and miracles. The way there is a courageous and joy-filled road. The time for blinders and superficiality is lost in illness, and we find ourselves with an opportunity to become real and self-connected. Divine Spirit embraces those who embrace that opportunity.

The self-healing energy exercises that follow are threefold in nature. They are designed to address the body, mind, and spirit. Some people use the term "creative visualization" to describe healing meditative states. In actuality, the vibratory and energetic experience of the meditative or healing state is not simply a visualization. It is a direct energetic experience that is real. If you do not yet understand this, it is fine to proceed with these exercises believing you will use your creativity and imagination to perform them. I will use the words "see," "do," and "feel" instead of "visualize," for in each of these exercises we are truly seeing, doing, and feeling on an energetic or vibratory level.

These energy exercises are generalized for the reader. If you have a specific illness or need, you can adapt the healing exercise to fit your needs. This is where education and awareness of your particular disease and healing process become important. For example, if you are undergoing chemotherapy or radiation designed to destroy cancer cells, you will be aware that these toxic processes also destroy and deplete healthy cells. Therefore, cleansing the toxins quickly from the body and beefing up the healthy cells with life force energy is important. If you have a chronic illness, such as Chronic Fatigue Syndrome, asthma, arthritis, or low back pain, there are specific areas of the body that require healing. Becoming familiar with your medical condition and the healing options you are employing, whether traditional or alternative or a combination thereof, will increase your awareness of what your body needs energetically.

Energy exercises are always used in conjunction with common sense. Depleted bodies require good nutrition including healthy food and fluids. Medication may be necessary. The more you are aware of the known facts or ideas regarding your illness or disease process, the more enlightened your healing efforts will be. In addition you may be surprised by information received during your energy exercises regarding your illness and healing. Be open to what emerges. It may indeed be a key to your healing.

A vast number of techniques, elements, and exercises may be employed to facilitate physical healing using energy. The nature of the illness or complaint and the ability of the individual to perform certain exercises influence what the practitioner is able to do. If one is extremely debilitated from the ravages of disease or chemotherapy, the level of physical energy one has to expend in energetic physical exercise is limited, but the spiritual healing exercises can be adapted to suit one's needs and abilities. This is the loving nature of spiritual energetic exercises. No matter what your physical condition, energy can be harnessed to facilitate physical, emotional, and spiritual healing. Self-healing exercises do not replace the beneficial healing energy an ill person needs from others. The exercises presented are those we can do for ourselves to promote self-healing while drawing on all other measures of healing we may need at a given time.

Self-healing exercises are not only for the ill. When we are in good health, the task of nurturing and maintaining that good health on all levels—physical, mental, and spiritual—and advancing or progressing in health and inner power can be accomplished by continuing on a path of practicing healing energy exercises. We are forever growing, expanding, and evolving; our inner healing journey follows us through our cycles.

The absolutely most important self-healing energy exercises are those that foster our inner connection to our own soul and fulfill our deepest spiritual longings and desires, thus granting joy and peace. We can embark upon spiritual life force exercises with the enlightened consciousness that our soul is who we truly are; our mind can consciously direct our soul's longings and our body exists to serve our mind and spirit. All are joined temporarily in this physical existence called life. With these metaphysical principles in mind, we can proceed along the path of practicing spiritual energy exercises that incorporate the body, mind, and soul.

Environment

Surroundings can serve healing. Nurturing, life-giving vibrational surroundings will enhance self-healing forces. If possible, have a place or space in your apartment, house, room, garden, or wherever you are that provides a soothing, aesthetically pleasing environment to facilitate your energy practices. If you are confined to a hospital room or bedridden, have some special objects, or pictures or flowers or plants that give you a visually pleasing and comforting physical focus. A nurturing environment can appeal to all of the senses. Try adding aromatically pleasing objects such as flowers, incense, or essential oils to your environment to facilitate energy practices. Often soothing music or sounds can be listened to when meditating or performing energy exercises. Or you can create your own sounds as in the sounding/vibrational energy exercises described in chapter 2. The senses and the vibrations associated with sound and music can be used to facilitate healing energetic states. Use technology to bring the outdoors in: the sounds of water falling, the tides along the beach, gentle drumming, the wind, and other natural sounds can all foster a healing environment.

We are seeking to build, create, or place ourselves in an environment that, even if momentary and temporary, will allow us some beauty, comfort, and inner quiet in which to practice our healing exercises. This need not be an elaborate or difficult process. There is beauty all around us. Nature offers numerous settings that can bring us a sense of comfort and beauty. The night sky, the roar of waves upon the beach, the blossoms of a tree outside our window, or the rays of sunlight that beam upon the earth can call us to our inner healing exercises. A simple, conscious tribute to the beauty around us is helpful and nurturing to the body, mind, and soul.

Position

Energy exercises can be done in any physical position: sitting, lying down, dancing, moving, swimming, and so on. There are no limits. If you are too ill to sit upright, lying down is fine. If you are not physically limited, there are times when you may choose to do healing energy exercises in many different situations, using a variety of postures or movements. The only restriction is that you do the exercises when awake. Energy exercises can be done prior to sleep, but the exercises that follow are conscious wakeful energy exercises for self-healing.

Self-Healing Energy Exercises

I have spoken of preparing your surroundings and providing a nurturing and soothing environment in which to do your healing energy practices. Now let us proceed to the different energy exercises you can learn and use for physical, emotional, and spiritual healing.

The following energy exercises combine the spiritual energy disciplines of meditation, prayer, and reflection (self-examination). They are designed to increase your awareness of your own body and to help you learn what its healing needs are and how you can send healing energy through it. You may emerge from the energy exercises with new insights and knowledge. Healing is a process, sometimes slow and arduous and sometimes quick. Be prepared for slow, steady gains and, of course, embrace the moment when favorable results occur.

Because attempting to focus on the chakra system can be confusing to many beginners in self-healing, the energy exercises that follow will bring a natural experience of the energy or chakra system to the practitioner without a lot of mental effort. These beginning self-healing energy exercises are like riding a bicycle, skiing, or any new activity. The basic dynamics, process, and mechanism can be cognitively learned, but until you do the activity you do not have a thorough kinesthetic understanding. And through practice, you can have a kinesthetic understanding without needing to understand the entire mechanism.

Prepare for these exercises in the following ways:

Prepare your environment or choose a space that offers optimal healing energy.

Allow yourself a minimum of fifteen minutes to practice these exercises.

Always position yourself comfortably.

Read the guided healing exercises several times in order to follow along in your practices. It is just fine to follow your own intuition and allow your healing energy exercise to flow into its own unique experience. The written exercises here are purely a framework from which to begin.

Upon ending the healing exercise you may desire to write down any significant experiences, images, insights, or awarenesses for further personal reference and remembrance.

Pine Forest

Make yourself comfortable in a seated or reclining position.

Begin your healing exercise by inviting your Higher Power or Divine Spirit to assist you in your healing efforts and affirm that Divine Guidance will assist you. Speak to Divine Spirit about that which requires healing. Tell Divine Spirit how you are feeling emotionally, spiritually, and physically. Be open and honest.

Close your eyes and bring your attention to your mind's eye. This is the inner place that is the entrance into spiritual vision. Once inside your mind's eye, see yourself sitting or lying in a quiet and wondrous pine forest. All around you are magnificent, towering pine trees. The ground upon which you rest is thickly padded with soft and aromatic pine needles, which have fallen from the trees. Immerse yourself in the gentle hush of the pine forest. Feel your body as it is connected to this beautiful, clean, and earthy place.

Breathe in the sweet fragrance of the pine forest. Absorb the stillness and life which surrounds you. Feel the energy of the earth and the pines, the strength and the quiet, as they rise up through your body. Allow the forest to fill you with its healing energy. See all the negative thoughts, aches, pains, lifeless energy, toxins, darkness, troubles, or illness begin to sink from your body and return to the earth. See and feel the continuous life force energy of the earth and pines fill your body with nourishing and cleansing strength. Continue to breathe in rejuvenating energy and breathe out all negativity.

As you fill your body, mind, and spirit with the pure gentleness of loving life force, see the unwanted and useless negative energy leave your body through your pores, your skin, your hands, your feet, and your exhaled breath. Watch as this negative energy is consumed and transformed by the overwhelming cleansing power of the forest and the earth. Continue to breathe in the positive life force energy and breathe out the negative.

When you feel full and clean and rested, sit still a moment and experience the loving vibrations that envelop you. Bless this beautiful place and time. Gently invite Divine Wisdom to bring you any message, image, or insight that would be helpful to you. Watch and listen in this quiet, light-filled place. Do not judge or censor what occurs. Simply observe and experience.

When you feel ready to leave this place and time, once again thank your Higher Power and the earth and the pines, and gently bring your consciousness back to the room in which you sit or recline. Stretch, yawn, relax, and enjoy.

Into the Body

Make yourself comfortable in a reclining position.

Invite Divine Spirit to assist you and enlighten you in your healing endeavor. Speak to your spiritual guidance about how you feel and what your perceived needs are.

Remember *The Fantastic Voyage?* In this healing exercise, you are going to travel inside your physical body. You will become a small version of yourself and journey through your own body.

Close your eyes and bring your focus to your mind's eye. As you begin to see a glowing ball of white light energy there, see a small you appear and step into the ball of radiant light. Slowly descend through your body to your right foot. See the bones, muscles, nerves, and circulatory system of your foot. Feel the energy there; note if there are aches or pains or if your foot is comfortable. Now travel up your right leg observing the internal workings and noticing what feels well or ill as you continue to travel up to the pelvis and course across it and over to your left leg. Travel down to your left foot. All the while the little you inside your own body is noting the feelings, experiences, and visual perceptions that occur. Again, travel up your left leg and into the pelvis. As you move upward observe your reproductive organs, your elimination and digestive systems, your heart and circulatory system, and your lungs. As you move up through your body, observe the internal organs, your spine, and neck. Travel across your shoulders, down your arms and hands then back to your mind's eye and your head.

Having made observations and experienced the areas of your body that may need healing energy, gather light energy into your little self from the brilliant glowing ball of light in your mind's eye. Become a little superhero, filled with light and power, who can direct healing light energy and vibration out from your little hands.

Travel back through your body. Go back to all the places you found that were in need of healing and loving energy. Guide that healing energy through your hands and touch all those places and fill them with this light energy.

After giving that energy to all the places that require healing, return to your mind's eye. Now see a great and beautiful light surrounding and enveloping you. Relax in its comfort and security. Breathe in this restful, nurturing light, and feel the cocoon of love that surrounds you. Note the color or colors of this cocoon of light. Rest within it for awhile.

When you are ready to emerge from your healing, gently bring your consciousness back to the room in which you recline. Breathe deeply, sigh, yawn, relax.

Healing Sands/Crystal Chamber

Make yourself comfortable in a reclining position.

Close your eyes. Invite Divine Spirit to be with you on your healing journey, and tell Divine Spirit who you are in this moment. Explain your thoughts, dreams, desires, and needs.

With eyes closed, bring your attention to your mind's eye. There you will see a window that opens on a beautiful, warm, and pleasant beach. Go through this window. Lie upon the sand and feel the warmth of the sun as it caresses you and the pulse of the deep sands upon which you rest. Continue to feel the sun and the sand, and hear the water that moves ceaselessly toward the shore. Immerse yourself in the sensations that surround and touch you.

Focus your attention on the life force of the sand that pulsates with the soft rhythm of the earth. Breathe in the fresh air, the sunlight, and the comfort of the sand upon which you rest, and breathe out all negativity, impurity, and unwanted energy. Allow the unwanted energy to leave your body and become cleansed as it sinks into the infinite sands beneath you. Continue to breathe in the nurturing life force energy of the sun, the water, and the sand.

When you feel full of life force energy and can feel the pulsating rhythm of the sand, see yourself gently sinking through the sand, deeper and deeper toward the earth's core. Move through the layers of sand, rock, earth, and clay. Feel each layer as it cleanses and fills your body with life force energy.

Continue your travel into the earth until you come upon a spectacular crystal chamber: a room of crystal walls with crystal stalagmites and stalactites. In this crystal room is a crystal healing bed upon which to rest and gather healing energy. Go there and rest awhile. Feel the vibrations of color and the laser energy of the living crystal room as it embraces and heals you with its energy. See the colors, the clarity, and the vibrations emanating through you and around you. Rest awhile here and listen, watch, and feel.

When you are ready to come back from your healing journey bring your consciousness back to the room in which you recline. Stretch, yawn, sigh, and tingle.

Healing Guardian

Make yourself comfortable in a reclining position.

Invite your Higher Power to help you and affirm that Divine Guidance supports you in your healing efforts. Speak to the Almighty about your present state and needs.

We all have spirit guardians, angels, or beings of light, which protect, guide, and direct us through life. Whether we know it or not or listen or not, they are ever present with us. In this healing exercise we are going to invite these loving beings to come and assist us in our healing.

Close your eyes and bring your focus to your mind's eye. Here, begin to see a brilliant rainbow of colors that spreads out and encompasses your entire body. Focus your attention on the beautiful rainbow colors as they radiate from your body and surround it. Invite your guardians to come and heal your body with their loving energy. Continue to focus on the rainbow colors and the loving energy you sense enveloping your body. Be aware of any beneficent and loving beings that may now surround you. You will feel an increasing sense of safety and comfort as your spirit guides begin to work on you. Observe and note where they bring healing energy to your body. Try to sense the love they have for you and absorb any messages they may bring to your attention. Fully relax as the loving colors, energy, and caring hands bring healing to you. Stay in this healing place as long as you need.

When you are ready to exit your healing session, lovingly thank your guides and bring your attention back to the room in which you recline. Stretch, relax, and enjoy.

Chakra Balancing

Stand or sit with your feet spread shoulder width apart, firmly on the floor. If you are standing bend your knees slightly. Keep your spine upright, head straight forward, and hands gently outstretched to the sides, if you are standing, or resting lightly on your knees, palms down, if seated.

Bring your attention to your feet and your first chakra area as depicted in Figure 1, chapter 2. If necessary, rotate your pelvis and move your feet and toes to facilitate the sense of your physical connection to the earth. Feel your feet and first chakra connecting deep down into the earth. Feel yourself sinking through the rich layers of the earth's crust and descending deep into the volcanic molten core of the earth. Feel the fiery energy of the earth's center as the red, the orange, the yellow, and blue-white flames of energy reach up through your feet and first chakra and fill your body and energy centers. Feel this energy as it rises up through your abdomen, spine, stomach, chest, throat, neck, and head. Feel this explosive energy as it emerges in golden white brilliance from the top of your head and beams up into the heavens in emanations of light, color, and vibration.

As you allow this energy to move through your system, close your eyes and attempt to see, feel, and experience its colors and vibrations, its ebbs and flows. Continue the exercise until you achieve a sense of comfort and balance, fullness and well-being.

When you are ready to exit this healing exercise, bring your awareness back to the room in which you are, and open your eyes. Breathe, stretch, relax.

This exercise will assist in balancing and filling your energy system. Once you start moving energy through your body, you are going to shift long-held energetic blocks and old experiences. If you allow the energy to flow through the entire system, it will be experienced in a more balanced manner. Allow the energy to flow all the way up through your crown chakra.

If you find that certain areas were blocked or the energy felt uneven, don't worry. Very few of us have perfectly balanced chakra systems.

Allow yourself time afterward to assess all your feelings—physical, emotional, and spiritual. You may wish to record your experiences if they were meaningful.

The River of Forgiveness

Just as the physical body needs healing energy exercises, so too do our emotional and spiritual bodies. This healing exercise is intended to free you from resentments, worries, fears, anger, or unnecessary guilt.

As in all the healing exercises, invite Divine Spirit to guide your efforts and bless your course.

Get comfortable in sitting or reclining position and close your eyes.

Focus your attention in your mind's eye and begin to see a beautiful path in a forest. You can hear the gentle running sound of a clear, sparkling brook. Follow the sound of the running water to the bank and walk slowly and quietly along the path on the brook's edge as it leads to the Great River. See the rocks along the brook's edge as you move toward the river, and feel the shade and sunlight as they dance upon the ground you walk on. Immerse yourself in the calm beauty of this solitary path.

In the distance, a jetty of earth juts out in perfect measure at the meeting place of the brook and the river. Go there and lie on the grassy earth where you can gaze comfortably out into the water. You can see your reflection in the mirror of the water. Be still and focus on the gently flowing water as it runs ceaselessly into the Great River and is swept out into the farthest reaches of the earth.

As you gaze into the water, see your fears float by one by one. See them, name them, and let them float away down the Great River. Then see the faces of those with whom you have difficulties; allow these faces to float away down the Great River. Allow your hurts and anger to float by in the clear, cool water. See all your worries, problems, resentments, and burdens float by you into the Great River.

When all these things have passed into the Great River and you feel calm, free, and unburdened, see a comfortable hammock suspended between the trees to the side of the path along which you came. Go to the hammock and lie restfully there. Listen to the sounds of the forest and the river. Rock peacefully back and forth and allow the cleansing, natural surroundings to heal your quiet soul.

When you are rested, bring your attention back to the room you are in and relax, stretch, enjoy.

You may wish to pray and give a blessing of thanks to Spirit.

Chapter 9

DREAMS, VISIONS, AND MIRACLES

Dreaming is a natural phenomenon for human beings. It is the doorway to the unconscious self. The dream world is a largely uninhibited and fascinating realm of the mind and spirit. Too few make use of the dream world as a place to actively develop spiritual energy and the inner connection to the larger reality of Divine Spirit. Just as the physical body contains within it the energy centers and life force line of our minds and spirits, the dream world is a gateway to the energetic/vibratory realms of consciousness. In fact, for many who are unable to access or see the other worlds of existence—those we call the spiritual worlds—in their conscious waking state, the world of dreams often will allow easier and more direct entrance to these realms without conscious effort. It is as if Divine Spirit anticipated the rational mind's denial of the spiritual world's existence and provided a mechanism by which all could easily participate in the collective unconscious and Divine Mind without actually having to exert much effort.

The dream world is a world within many worlds just as our vibratory natures are multidimensional. In the vibrational world of dreams, the unconscious self can process and explore many daily events and life experiences without the inhibitions of the rational mind. The rational mind is most often asleep in the world of dreams and the unconscious or unrepressed and free self can fly here.

There are many states and levels of dreaming, just as there are different levels of meditation, self-examination, and prayer. The most frequent level of dreaming processes the thoughts, feelings, and experiences of our daily life as we sleep. This standard processing of dreaming naturally occurs within each dream cycle. These dreams can be disturbing, enlightening, or nonmemorable. They are the dreams we need to dream to process that which energetically requires inner processing. These dreams can offer much information about our inner processing of events if we can recall them in the conscious or waking state. Often they can reveal to us our innermost and buried feelings and thoughts regarding events of our lives. They can reveal our fears, desires, and longings. These dreams, if recalled, can serve to illustrate for us what our unconscious ingeniously does to call us to heed the deeper self.

Dreams demonstrate how remarkable the unconscious is in offering us messages that the waking mind may be blind or resistant to. Dreams can facilitate our growth in the areas of self-examination, meditation, and prayer, and these spiritual disciplines can facilitate deeper, purposeful, and more easily recalled dreams. One can become a more conscious dreamer. That is not to say that we wish to control our dreaming, although that is quite possible at times, but rather that we learn to allow our unconscious a more open and direct channel to our conscious minds.

Recalling dreams allows our unconscious minds to speak to us and guide us in the waking state.

There are some dreams that are more significant or powerful to the dreamer than others. These can be dreams that reflect a life passage or developmental milestone in soul progression or dreams that are enlightening, healing, prophetic, and/or spiritual in nature. We can access other realms in dreams and often can be with those who have passed from physical life to spiritual form. The dream world is a direct entrance to other realms of reality and existence. Here Divine Spirit can speak to us and we are more open to listening without the ever censoring and controlling conscious mind monitoring the celestial gates.

Dreaming with spiritual purpose is, in fact, an art or mystical practice. It is also an energetic spiritual practice. There are means to improve one's ability to recall dreams, dreams with directed purpose, and dreams with increased spiritual learning.

The dream world offers one the ability to come to know the self on more profound levels. Healers, mystics, and wise people consider the dream world as important a place of soul evolvement as the physical reality. The dream world actually offers the human being the experience of the world of spirit without consciousness of the body. It brings us closer to our spiritual essence than the physical world. It is a very powerful place for receiving knowledge, communicating with Spirit, and developing the soul.

I have said that the dream world exists on many vibratory/energetic levels. These levels incorporate the darker realms or underworld of the soul as well as the angelic or celestial realms. Both serve immense purpose for humanity: the dream world only reflects the spiritual levels of soul evolvement present within and among us. The darker or murkier world of dreams is not to be feared as a place of unlearning. We all possess (unless we are totally enlightened perfect beings) a darkness and a lightness of being. We are human. We live in an external world where the best and worst of humanity exist. We also live in an internal world which is not free of conflicts, struggles, and some darkness.

This darkness can be self-doubt, guilt, pain, life experiences that were not for our greatest good, secrets, fears, or what we judge to be sins. It is a place of unenlightenment, yet a place that can bring tremendous light to the soul. For when we understand that we can travel through this darkness with Divine Spirit as our guide we can own, incorporate, digest, and join the darkness to the light of our own souls, or eradicate aspects of the darkness. We are, in fact, reclaiming the lost self and bringing the unworthy or dark places of our being back to the source of light and Spirit. We can absorb the darkness to become whole and one with the eternal light.

Most students of self-healing and spiritual practice do not shun or cut themselves off from their own darkness or the darkness of the world. They bring the darkness to the light. For really what in truth are we trying to heal? We are trying to heal those places within us and without us that appear to lack light. We would not be much as healers if we were only willing to stay in places of abundant love. We would be living in isolation and not doing the rest of the world much good by not sharing our light.

Likewise, we can't cut ourselves off from our darker sides. We want to bask in and absorb the supernal light and love of Divine Spirit, and we would do well to share it with our darker self. It is not a bad self. It is a self that requires incorporation and oneness. So we learn to walk through the dream underworld with power. We carry the lamp of understanding and Divine Spirit with us. We do not go alone and we need not go in fear. If it is within us it is ours to explore.

The levels of the dream world also include levels of increasing light, vibration, and color. They traverse all the realms of spirit we can reach with our hearts, and souls. In dreams we can experience glorious, shining, and magnificent worlds of luminescent color, vibration, and sound. We can travel through the realms of mind and spirit to greet the Angels of Divine Wisdom. We can enjoy the gifts of knowledge of universal mind and join with the Eternal Love that surrounds and is one within us. The world of dreams is a well of spiritual fortune. If we drink deeply we can proceed to further enlightenment.

Our dreams can become a guide in everyday life. They offer symbols and signposts and clear messages to the conscious self. There are simple practices to assist us in learning to become avid and able dream weavers and dream receivers.

We have already explored three energy disciplines that augment the dream cycle. Meditation begins the process of moving vibration and energy through all states of awareness and being. It is a discipline that fosters the mingling of unconscious and conscious soul awareness. It is a discipline of light, vibration, sound, movement, and color. By joining us in conscious connection to the Divine Spirit, meditation accelerates the unfoldment of conscious connection between the physical and spiritual realms.

Self-examination in the presence of a mentor, psychotherapist, or one skilled in the art of dream interpretation can become a richer and more revealing spiritual practice with the use of dream work. Once the commitment to truthful and open self-examination is consciously made, dreams become clearer and easier to recall. In addition, those who are skilled at dream interpretation can teach us how to interpret our own dreams with improved insight. Many times, in the process of sharing a dream with another, the meaning of the dream crystallizes.

Prayer is the grand opener for guidance and dreams of power and soul evolvement. Prayer prior to the dream cycle evokes Divine Spirit and Wisdom to nurture and guide our dreams. Sweet surrender to a power greater than ourselves is beneficent and kind. In prayer, we can enter the dream world in the comfort of Divine Presence, knowing that with Divine Love to guide us, everything will unfold exactly as it should. Through the darkness or through the realms of immense light we go whence our Father bids to learn of ourselves and come home again.

Dream journals, logs, or diaries can assist the dream student. Recalling dreams while still in the state of dream fuzziness upon awakening is a good practice to help us better remember our dreams. When waking is a softer experience, the art of dream remembering is easier. You can actually slip back into dream consciousness to recall pieces, symbols, or parts of the dream. Of course there are very powerful dreams that are not forgotten and seem to be imprinted in your memory.

Whatever the level of your dream recall or dream abilities, they can be improved with spiritual disciplines and effort. In addition, proper nutrition, adequate rest and exercise, and avoidance of the excesses of alcohol and drugs will facilitate meaningful dream work.

There are many books and teachings on the subject of dream work and dream interpretation. I always feel that if something feels right or works for you then do it. There is much to learn about the worlds of dreams and the best guide is your own soul.

Through spiritual energy practices, a healer learns how to facilitate waking dream states as well as participate in the unconscious dream world as a conscious or aware being. Conscious participation in the unconscious world of dreams allows healers to influence their own healing or the healing of others. This is really no different than Spirit coming into your own dreams to influence, inform, or offer healing to you.

We are, in fact, spiritual beings and there are those among us who know this and are aware that with Divine Guidance they can enter dreams. Sometimes these people are referred to as shamans, mystics, gurus, or healers. Sometimes these people include you. Through love and energy connections to others, especially those we love, we show up in one another's dreams. We can speak to, influence, or give messages to one another. I am sure that many of you have experienced a dream in which there was a vivid communication between two souls who meant or mean much to each other. It can have occurred as a natural process of two souls connected to one another. In the shamanic or healer's world, conscious dreaming to assist in revelation and soul healing is a spiritual practice. It is a way toward soul evolvement and divine connection. For most though, dreaming is a way toward healing and revealing the self. As people who desire truer connection to their own souls and life purpose the dream world is a wondrous place. To honor the self is to honor the unconscious as well as the conscious. We can therefore honor our dreams as a place of spiritual unfoldment and inner healing.

Because I am a student of the metaphysical healing arts, dream work is very essential to my development both personally and professionally. There are those who have an ability to dream in certain circumstances as the designated group dreamer. These are individuals who are easily teachable in the dream state and therefore open to receive a group dream. What is a group dream? In a gathering of people—whether a family or a community—there are dreams or messages that are directed to the entire group. The group dreamer is the representative of the group in the dream world. The group dreamer is merely a portal through which Spirit can speak to a group in a dream. Naturally, the dreamer can have obvious personal attachment to the dream itself, just as the dreamer has attachment to the group. I, and many other "sensitives" I know, can consciously or unconsciously key into our soul grouping connections through the world of dreams. Many of you can, too. Perhaps your dreams may have already pre-informed you of the feelings or circumstances of family members or close relations prior to the next day's telephone call. All minds are joined and accessible in the dream world. Those deep connections which bind us to one another are available. With the guidance of Divine

Spirit we can learn to listen and communicate with those we love in the dream world.

It appears that the dream world just keeps opening the doors of possibility for spiritual communication and learning. And so it does. From this world of dreams we can better learn about ourselves and Divine Spirit and better learn about our fellow humans.

To become a self-healing dreamer, ask for Spirit's guidance before each dream cycle. Continue all your spiritual energy disciplines in wakefulness or consciousness. You will soon be able to sort out the digestion of life events from the pointedness of spiritual messages. With your efforts and the assistance of a Higher Power and another person, your dreams will reveal much wisdom to your conscious mind.

It has been said and written that many great people have received inspiration for their work and discovered answers to their questions in their dreams. There are cultures where dreaming was integral to the form of its members' creative work in the world. Dreaming was the inspiration for the creative process. The phrase "let me sleep on it" is really more accurately worded "let me dream on it." This attributes the power of processing and receiving answers to the world of dreaming.

Daydreams are very often marvelous passages of time wherein we let our minds wander to where they desire to be. Daydreams can be pleasurable respites in a grueling daily schedule. Creative visualization is a form of daydreaming wherein we actively or consciously choose our dream and affirm its real ability to manifest materially in our life. We can practice this form of dreaming in the meditative conscious state and vibrationally tune in to energy of universal consciousness. Daydreams and night dreams can serve parts of ourselves that hunger for expression and provide respite and wisdom to our souls.

Healing Dreams and Answers from Spirit

I will now share with you dreams of healing, of personal growth, and of messages from Divine Spirit. The world of dreams is an interwoven network of many realms of reality and therefore any dream can occur on many levels. The dreams I have selected to share here are those in which I have participated as a healer or as a student of dreams or those that were shared with me for interpretation or guidance.

Touched by the Hand of God

In one of my work places I was approached by a co-worker named Samantha who appeared anxious and slightly embarrassed as she came into the rehabilitation office. The office was full of several other co-workers at the time and as the healing work I am involved in is common knowledge amongst many of the staff, Samantha stated openly that she had had a dream that she would like me to interpret for her. She went on to describe this dream, which included her presence as well as that of her children, and told me that in the dream she had been struck by lightning. She was very afraid of what this meant.

I could clearly see how frightened she was and how very much she wanted an answer. As there was a crowd of onlookers in the room, I decided not to tell her the sacred meaning of the dream at that moment because it was not the proper environment in which to honor the sacredness of the message that was given. Instead I pulled out a dream book that was handy and looked up lightning in the book for her and read it to her. It was not the full or personal message she was to be given. I told her I would meditate on it further and see if I could divine more meaning from the dream. I already knew what the dream meant. This was just a way for me to await a more proper and quiet moment to share the true meaning with her.

Later in the day, I went up to Samantha's office. She was workir.g with another who was in her office. I went in and asked if she would like to know the further meaning of her dream and she said she would and that it was okay to share it with her in the presence of this co-worker. I explained to her that she had in fact been touched by the hand of God and that this message to her was that she was not forgotten by him. She began to cry, for this message meant so much to her.

Her husband was gravely ill with a liver disease that had progressed so rapidly that without a liver transplant his hopes of living much longer were dim. These were relatively young people who had young children and, of course, the past year or more had tried their courage and faith. She told me she had prayed to God for a message of some kind for quite some time and believed very devoutly in the love of God.

I had never had much intimate interaction with this co-worker before although there was always friendliness between us. I knew her to be a hardworking, down-to-earth and good human being. There is such immense love in the sharing of a deep truth of the soul that I felt her relief and gratitude in the awakened knowledge that she did not walk alone, that her God was with her.

Within twenty-four hours of her dream, her husband received a call for a transplant. His course of surgery and recovery was complicated by many factors. This first transplant did not work and he had to await yet another liver. To be offered one liver is a miracle, to receive a second liver within the time needed to sustain life was another miracle. The hand of God had touched this family's life. The days of healing and recovery ahead were likely to be long and arduous, but the gifts were clear. In this woman's dream was a spiritual message that preceded the miraculous gift given to them.

The Ancient Healing Temple

There was a young woman who was scheduled to undergo surgery requiring general anesthesia. She was very frightened of the surgery, not so much of the procedure but of the general anesthesia. The prospect of being totally helpless and reliant on the skill and care of others for her very breath was terrifying. As this young woman was of a spiritual path and a practitioner of spiritual energy disciplines, she prayed, meditated, and self-examined regarding the issue of her illness and the issue of the surgery. She had no trouble having faith in God and in herself, but she very definitely had trust issues with others. The night before her surgery she prayed and meditated prior to sleep and had a dream of healing.

This young woman found herself inside an ancient system of temples that was used for healing the ill as well as for the training and residence of the healers or priesthood of the time. There were outer and inner chambers in the temple. Only those who were to be granted healing by the priesthood were allowed to enter into the inner healing chambers. This young woman was to receive a healing because of her illness and was allowed passage into the inner sanctum.

As the young woman entered the inner chamber she was overcome by the divine love and beauty that resided therein. She was filled with a sense of peace, comfort, and nurturance that she had not before known. She lay down upon a table and a spirit guide whom she recognized from meditations appeared next to her and began to work on her. He was a barefoot Chinese doctor who was a surgeon and herbal medicine man as well as an energy healer. He was not a part of the temple system culture by his very nature.

As her physician surgeon/spirit guide worked on her with skill and compassion she succumbed to the beauty and peace and allowed herself to slip into the total support she felt there. One thought crossed her mind: why can you only enter here if you are sick or a part of the royal priesthood? It was so lovely here, it should be open to all. She drifted into unconsciousness knowing she was being healed.

When she awoke the next morning, a calm that was not her own possessed her. It was as if she was in a serene and pleasant trance that even daily activities such as brushing her teeth and driving to the hospital could not break. Her friend who drove her to the hospital also seemed overtaken by this calm, and they walked in surreal comfort to the surgical suite entrance. Her blood pressure was taken, a perfect 110/60 just prior to her stretcher ride to the surgery suite. The calm and peace continued as the surgical team prepped her for surgery. Just before she slipped under anesthesia she informed the entire surgical team "I love you all" with the most peaceful and serene smile on her face.

This young woman recovered without incident and knew that through the healing world of a dream she had been given the drug of calm surrender prior to an experience that could have been traumatic but instead was soul-healing. She had gone to a higher level of trust within herself and in the fellowship of humankind. She had not been deserted in her time of need. She had seen the inner temple and experienced its love. She had been met by one of her spirit guides and given the healing before the physical surgery.

The only thing that bothered her was the system of keeping from the temple common people who were neither ill nor of priesthood. So she went to her earth healing teacher and shared her anger at this unjustness. Her mystical teacher gazed at her in a serious and penetrating manner with a look of obvious consternation (as in, you should know this already) and said to her, "But the temple gates are open now." Old anger at inequities of the past is fruitless. It is now as it should be. The temple gates on earth are open to all. None can bar the way and we needn't be sick or of the privileged class to be allowed to rest in the healing energy of Divine Love.

A Self That Was Ready to Die

Kate was a woman who had worked earnestly at her spiritual energy disciplines for over thirteen years. She had battled the darker places of her life—her youthful addictions and dysfunctional psychological patterns—to emerge victorious in surrender to her spiritual path and to live according to her soul's truth. Kate's life was a reflection of her joyous path. She was to marry the man she loved and had lived with for over six years, and her work in the world was the direct extension of her spiritual path. Life could not have been more promising or fulfilling. But her world came crashing in three days before her wedding. During a phone conversation with her parents, Kate discovered that they would not be able to participate in her wedding ceremony in the way they had promised more than ten months prior. All of a sudden, they could not bear the fact that the religious ceremony planned was not of their faith. Instead they would be willing to attend the wedding but not walk Kate down the aisle together as planned or stand with both families and the bridal party upon the bimah (altar). This was unacceptable to Kate whose happiness was being sabotaged at the last minute by her parents who had for the past six years appeared to embrace both Kate and her groom as part of the family.

Over the years the religious aspect of Kate's marriage had been discussed with her parents thoroughly and clearly. Kate's parents, though understandably saddened by their daughter's religious choice, had expressed their acceptance and appeared to offer their congratulations and support. This being the case, Kate was totally unprepared for and shocked by the turnabout in the wedding plans.

Kate did something that finally demonstrated her emotional health and respect for herself. She told her parents that she expected them to come and be the parents of the bride that day as they had initially promised and if they could not do that then not to come at all. There would not be any sabotage or obvious public display of behavior that would shift all the attention from the joy of the day to the bereaved parents sitting in the background. There had been adequate and proper time for her parents to have told Kate of their changed minds. Now they could come as planned or not come at all. They chose not to come and to miss their daughter's wedding day.

On her honeymoon Kate had a dream that would reveal itself to be a healing brought through the unconscious mind. In this marker dream Kate would move to a much richer and more open place within.

In the dream, Kate found herself on the darkened canals of Venice. She saw a young woman dressed in the fashion of her adolescent years. The young woman was wearing go-go boots, a miniskirt, and a nehru-collared shirt. She was standing on top of a Venetian building with the intention of committing suicide. Kate was extremely distraught at seeing the young woman who was about to take her own life and ran to a group of people gathered at a sidewalk café to enlist help. Kate pleaded with the group to help her save the girl, but they just looked at her unemotionally and said that the girl wanted to die. Kate couldn't believe their lack of concern. Then she saw her husband. She asked him to help save the girl, too, but even he did not respond as she wished. He even held Kate back from going to the girl.

The young woman then leaped to her death and lay on the street, neck broken and lifeless. Kate went over to her and saw a peaceful smile on the girl's face.

"She wanted to die." The unemotional and firm response rang in Kate's ears. It was as if to have interfered with this girl's choice would have been wrong. Kate could not believe that no one but herself had wanted to save the girl and yet even Kate had not moved to keep the young woman from her death. It did somehow appear to be a personal choice that should not have been prevented.

Kate awoke from her dream in the middle of the night crying loudly and in distress. Her husband awakened and listened to Kate's dream in his semiconscious state. He reassured her and returned to sleep. Kate eventually fell back to sleep as well, but the vivid memory of the dream stayed with her.

Upon Kate's return from the honeymoon she called upon her self-examination teacher who is an excellent dream interpreter. Kate told her of the dream. Kate's concern was that possibly she was even more distressed than she consciously knew because Kate herself had never considered suicide as a life option and was worried that her unconscious self was telling her that she was considering it. This was a chilling thought especially since it did not jibe with Kate's conscious feelings. She was very obviously shattered emotionally by the betrayal and abandonment she had recently undergone, but suicide was extreme.

Being outside the dream and the dreamer, Kate's wise mentor lightly wiped away that fear. The young woman in the dream was a part of Kate, a part dressed in the fashion of Kate's adolescent and teen years. The young woman represented a time in Kate's life history that was fraught with pain and dysfunction. She was a Kate who did not know who she was and was filled with anxiety and uncertainty. She was a Kate who had not had many choices or options for help out of her dysfunction. She was a Kate who did not exist anymore. This self was ready to die.

Kate could now let go of the young woman who had little power, few choices, and lived in constant fear. She could open that space for the woman she had become. Her inner world had become larger and she could now give healthy nurturance and unconditional love to herself. Her world was full of personal courage and choices. Kate's dream was a healing marker dream, which is a dream that marks a significant life-growth event for the soul. Kate had changed. For now if any choose to stay or be in a relationship with Kate, it will be with the woman she is, not with the fear-filled child she was. The woman she is now has the power and courage to demand the dignity, respect, and honor she deserves.

Bread with Honey

I often pray prior to sleeping to be able to help or assist those I love in the dreamtime if they should need some help. On one such evening I particularly prayed for all the children in my life whom I love very much. That evening as I dreamed, I was interrupted in my dream by the shrieking cry of terror of a child's voice. I immediately knew it was Bonnie. I went to the sound of the voice and located Bonnie who was in a dark, dark place like a tunnel or playground tunnel with her younger sister. She was terrified. I soothed her and told her she was not alone and that everything was all right. When she appeared comforted and calm, I left the children and went back into my own dream. Again, I heard piercing shrill cries from the little girl. This time I went back, turned on all the lights, and called all the other children I knew to the playground. I gave all the children bread with honey and we all sang songs and danced and laughed. I stayed with the children.

Upon waking the next morning I was concerned about Bonnie. I speak to her parents, old friends since childhood, very infrequently as years and life changes have grown between us. However the nudging that I call to find out about the child would not abate. My concern for the little girl was too strong to allow her parents' possible ridicule of me for my "psychic" work to dissuade me from calling. It is not that Bonnie's parents do not love me; they do, but their careers and natures do not lend themselves to the practice of energy phenomena. They are of the more pragmatic and rational-minded persuasion.

When I called, my old friend picked up the phone, and I launched in. "Hi, I know this is kind of unusual, but I had a dream about Bonnie last night and was wondering how she is." My friend defensively asked, "What kind of dream?" I was startled by the strong reaction but went on to describe the dream in full. Silence followed, then, in a softened voice my friend explained, "Yesterday Bonnie did not want to go to bed because of a nightmare she keeps having. I asked her to tell me the dream and she said she couldn't because that would make it happen again. I assured her that if she told me the dream it would most probably make it better. She conceded and told me the nightmare. It was the exact dream you just described to me and she was with her younger sister. They were all alone and afraid. Upon Bonnie's waking this morning I asked her how she had slept and she said, 'Fine, Daddy.'"

I did not need to say too much more to my friend. I was just glad his little girl was okay.

And so it is with the dream world. We can do our spiritual work there guided by a force greater than ourselves.

I have often gone to sleep after giving a spiritual or soul question to Spirit for assistance and have awakened with the answer after a beautifully choreographed vibrational dream experience which enlightened me. Entrusting one's soul to Divine Spirit prior to sleep is a practice we teach our children. Let us not forget the power of that practice in adulthood.

Healing Dream Techniques

The basic healing principles of meditation, prayer, and reflection can be used to dream with increased awareness and to facilitate self-healing through dreams. Proper amounts of regular sleep and good health habits are also beneficial. The exhausted are too tired to dream effectively. The stressed-out and depressed have sleep and dream difficulties. These situations require care when you are awake if you are to become an effective conscious dreamer.

Prayer and meditation facilitate sleep. They also facilitate Higher Power-directed dreaming. Prior to sleep reflect on your day. This is a time for a mini stock-taking or simply a spiritual review. Consider the day's events, the pluses, the minuses, and where you may have been emotionally, spiritually, and so on. If you speak to Divine Spirit earnestly and sincerely about where you are and where you wish to go or what you would like to learn in the dream world you will be readily answered. Requests to Divine Spirit rarely go unanswered. It is we who do not remember those answers.

The best way to start out is to surrender to Spirit Guidance prior to sleep. Here is an example of a dream prayer:

"Dear Great Spirit, in your love I entrust my dream lessons. May I be a good student and learn that which you teach me tonight in the dream world. May I remember that which you wish for me to consciously know. Good night my Dearest Father, in your arms I rest my soul."

You may have specific requests or journeys you wish to make in dreams: ask for them. You will be amazed at the results. Whether your requests are for healings or for answers to life situations or vexing problems, entrust them to Spirit and ask for enlightenment in the dream world. Spirit is generous, kind, and easily accessible in dream time when you are more open.

There will be nights when you simply need to fall asleep. Each and every night, if you make it a habit to entrust your sleep and dreams to God, that which is meant to flow will flow. The necessary processing of life events, emotions, situations, inner feelings, and unconscious thoughts will continue to unravel in the world of dreams. Dreaming is the emotional equivalent of the digestive and elimination systems of the body. It is, in itself, healing and cathartic. There are dreams that are the regular and necessary processing of events, and then there are dreams that show mysteries revealed and truths uncovered, which are deeply meaningful and spiritual. All these dreams are important to us. For they all offer us healing and information.

I usually do a daily self-review, meditation, and prayer prior to sleep. If I have a specific problem, request, thank you, or blessing, I offer it to Spirit for Divine Wisdom.

I do not attempt to direct my dreaming each night. Spirit knows better than I what I need to learn and experience. However, there are times when I have an earnest request and am sincerely focusing on a specific soul issue, goal, or relationship. At these times I may indeed focus my energy or will in a specific request to Spirit and I have always been answered. Try it. If you truly desire a response, it will come.

A mystical helper or simply another tool that facilitates dreaming is a glass of water by your bedside. When you awaken in the morning if you did not drink your water in the night, do not drink your dream water: it is of yesterday and of the already dreamed. Get yourself a fresh clean glass of water to drink in the morning. Water energetically calls forth our spirit nature and enhances dream catharsis.

Recording dreams often helps us to interpret them with increased astuteness. Therefore keeping a dream journal is helpful. Write down your dreams first thing upon waking. In the semi-wakefulness between sleep and full consciousness, you are better able to remember your dreams.

There are many books on dream symbols and the meanings of dreams. Keeping a journal and consulting a dream dictionary can help get you into the habit of remembering your dreams and interpreting them. As mentioned previously, often in sharing a dream with another trusted and beloved soul, the meaning crystallizes instantly. There are many excellent psychotherapeutic dream interpreters. The journal and dictionaries are tools to assist you in remembering and understanding dreams. The dreams that haunt you, inspire you, and impart revelation or spirit communication are usually relatively simple to understand. They are also easily recalled.

The most exciting aspects of learning how to become a dream weaver are the worlds of consciousness, knowledge, and wisdom we can enter through the dream world. We can go on magical journeys, and venture into the past, the future, the timeless, the eternal.

We can continue our soul's growth and self-discovery in dream time. We can meet our spirit guides, loved ones, and be with Divine Spirit. The world of dreams is a world of infinite learning and opportunity. Ask each night and what you need to know shall be revealed. It really is just that simple.

Visions and Visitations

To speak of visions and visitations by Divine Spirit and those who are called spiritual beings is to enter the realm of consciousness that recognizes ourselves as spiritual beings. We are connected to Divine Spirit and capable of receiving communication that transcends the physical reality in which we normally participate. In biblical and religious history, we come upon references to figures who frequently sought, through their faith and devotions, to be visited by Divine Presence. We also find many accounts of people who were visited by Divine Presence and whose lives were changed by the event. Such historical recordings teach us that this phenomenon is ancient and common amongst all religious cultures. We often hear the words "rapture," "ecstasy," "bliss," and "sanctification" associated with the state of being visited by the Divine Presence. Prophets and holy people through the ages have attributed their revelations and visions to the experience of union, however brief, with Divine Spirit.

This is not to say that Divine Spirit will only present itself to a person who is totally enlightened or to one of the great prophets. That would be sad indeed, as most of us would acknowledge. No, in fact, Divine Presence is so beneficent that it extends its love to all and will reveal itself in its own time and manner to those who will listen. There are levels of communion or contact with Divine Spirit just as there are levels of soul development. The opportunity to embrace and receive these divine experiences comes from devotion to spiritual practices and living life in a manner that regards all life as joined. But the experience of Divine Visitation is not controlled by us. The best we can do as children of God is to show up and present ourselves through our spiritual devotions in a consistent and focused manner and we will perhaps be granted this gift of Divine Grace when Divine Presence chooses to reveal itself to us.

The level of divine connection of the individual soul to the Creator I am speaking of is one which cannot be forced by human will nor does it depend on the human spirit's time frame. It is beyond our control. The very occurrence of such a transcendent and holy experience demonstrates our relationship to the Creator. We are birthed in the All and All and we are the created. In our surrender to this truth shall we know the Almighty.

There are those elevated human souls whose personalities were/are entirely merged with the larger reality and in continual oneness with Divine Mind. They are few indeed and walk in this Divine Union with the Holy Presence in achieved perpetuity. This however is not the state of most of us and yet we can work to become more aligned with Divine Presence through our lives. We are all loved equally by the Divine Creator even if we don't know it. In awakening our spiritual consciousness and remembering the truth of who we are in ever increasing daily moments we come closer toward walking the path of those who are merely more awakened than we are. Visions can be given to us all. Do the spiritual work and the gifts will follow. If you are given through grace the vision of oneness with the Divine Presence, it is solely due to the compassion and love the Creator extends to us all even in our forgotten sleep. So let us awaken our hearts, minds and spirits to the oneness and unity of ourselves and our relationship to God. In this devotion and one-mindedness we come closer to realizing the peace of God.

What is a vision? The word implies a picture or visual experience. As mentioned before, visions can be experienced on many levels. In meditation and prayer, visions can become part of the meditative or prayerful experience. Visions are energetic spiritual experiences that most often incorporate more than just a visual experience. A vision can be a totally encompassing state in which all the human and spirit systems within actually are transported to a realm of divine beauty and supreme life force energy. This is experienced by the receiver as a state of rapture, bliss, holiness, and joy that incorporates every fiber and awareness of his or her being. It is a transformation from the physical reality to the eternal reality with the delight of Divine Union mesmerizing the soul. The receiver is transfixed by the glory of the truth of holiness. These visions can be of the worlds closer to the physical world or of the higher natural worlds of spiritual existence that are closer to the Source.

There are worlds within spiritual existence as there are levels of soul evolvement and spiritual awakening. We can regularly visit and be a conscious part of many of the worlds of spiritual existence, but those closest to the Source are more difficult to enter. This is mainly because our consciousness does not yet allow us to enter here but also because sustained conscious awareness in the Living Place of God would render the physical life unnecessary. Therefore most of us are granted glimpses of the eternal realms closest to the Source of all light only momentarily, for we have much spiritual work to do to evolve back to this dwelling place.

We are given visionary gifts and direct visionary access to the realms of spirit that can bring to us great learning. So if you speak with the angels, receive visits from sage spirits, or hear the voice for truth within your soul, you are visionary. All of us can achieve some level of spiritual vision which propels us forward in our soul's spiritual evolvement. When you begin to undergo these experiences you will come to understand the different levels of experience I am speaking of. There are moments of perfect clarity, of knowledge, of spirit or beloved visitation, of energy transmittance through your body and consciousness, of soul messages or revelatory personal wisdom. The levels of spiritual experience are endless. A joyous loving embrace by Divine Spirit that comforts you throughout the day is a level of a visionary experience. Through the darkness and difficulty of life, we can most certainly actively participate in spiritual energy practices that bring spiritual vision. It is up to us to show up for the experiences that await.

On my spiritual path I have come across many who have enjoyed the visions that Spirit brings to us. As one who has practiced the spiritual disciplines for awhile, I have had many such visionary experiences. There are levels of spiritual vision which I now enter easily because of my spiritual energy practices. Healing, speaking with or seeing those who have passed from physical form, and traveling into the celestial realms becomes easy for the diligent practitioner. But there are visionary experiences that I cannot through my own efforts choose whether or when to enter. I have had visions which were given as a gift of Spirit and are the most powerful spiritual experiences I have known in this lifetime. I did not choose the time or place for these experiences and indeed I considered myself to have been less evolved in spiritual nature when these events actually occurred in my life. I do not question the mind of God in his choice and offering of these experiences to me. I only know that when they occurred I was extremely confused in my outer life although totally focused on my devotion and surrender to a Higher Power.

The following two experiences occurred within the same year and were unlike any visions I have experienced before or since. I have often prayed to experience them again, for the power, beauty, and joy of them is only touched on in moments in my regular spiritual practices. But because of these experiences I have gone on to levels of awareness and knowledge that are for me miraculous, joyful, and ever unfolding. I also know this: the place to whence I am going is the place I most want to be. There is nothing that can compare to it and there is nothing else. It is home and I cannot understand why we ever left. Nor will I waste more time figuring that piece out. All I know is I want to go home and I must bring all my brothers and sisters with me. We all must go home together, for if one is left behind, we are all left behind.

I will attempt to share with you one such vision, but it may be difficult to understand fully because when we enter the higher realms of consciousness, language becomes such a poor conveyor of actual experience. I wish to share it with you for it was a vision of extraordinary importance in my life. I once shared it with a now-popular lecturer on miracles and she must have been very moved by it for to my surprise one day I popped on one of her lecture tapes and heard my vision being used by this spiritual lecturer to bring the listeners into a meditative and prayerful state. It was strange to hear her voice tell the vision to an audience, and yet to hear it used to induce meditation and assist in prayerfulness and joining with God was beautiful. So here is the origin of the vision that is now known by many who have listened to it in a lecture on miracles.

One evening during a period in my life when I was confused and unclear as to my direction, I retired for sleep in the manner I was practicing at the time by doing a meditation and a prayer. I was very involved at this time in a specific metaphysical path that teaches about miracles and it was the one thing I was doing with pure devotion and purpose amidst all the confusion and pain in my life. It is very essential to note here that I was not under the influence of drugs or alcohol. I have never been diagnosed as psychotic or delusional. I present this here to rule out any implication that the experience was anything other than what it was: a visit with God.

In the most vivid awakening of all my senses and in the brilliance of celestial song and light I saw before me in the distance a vision of greater splendor and beauty than I have ever known. There was a woman who was cupped in living golden hands. She was wearing a white gown and lying on her stomach with her elbows bent and her inner forearms resting upon the Living Golden Hands with her neck and head reaching upward in transfixed rapture to receive the light, love, and beauty that came upon her. As I watched this scene I was overcome by the beauty of this woman. She was the most beautiful creature I have ever seen. As I looked at this vision, I began moving toward it and all at once the woman was me. I was in these golden living hands, drinking in the glory of being in the hands of God. There was an overwhelming joy, peace, life force, and ecstasy that was perfect.

There is no experience of the flesh that is possible to compare with this blissful place, for here in the hands of God there were no needs. All was full: I wanted nothing and was filled with everything. I lay back and basked in the total peace and completeness which enveloped and fulfilled me. A song of the angels and celestial vibration filled every cell and fiber of my being. I wanted to remain forever in this peace and bliss and glorious life energy.

As soon as I had this thought, I was traveling back away from this place, back toward my room and consciousness of being in bed. I was totally awake and looked down at myself in the bed. I was lying prone on elbows with my hands flat against the mattress, just as the woman had been in the vision. My head and neck had been gently outstretched and reaching upward when I came back to the consciousness of the room. I was in a state of sustained energetic trance but totally aware of what had just occurred and where I had been. I wanted to go back; there was a part of me that was saddened that I was here again, yet the joy of knowing where I had been and by what I had been touched made me radiate gratitude and wonder.

To be with God is to know oneness and completeness, a state where there is nothing but bliss and fullness. We know only eternal and increasing love and abundance. We want for nothing and have no needs. All is given and received. This was not a mere visual experience; it was a total immersion of body, mind, and consciousness in a sea of endless loving, living Divine energy that is home to every soul. For me, it was the dwelling place of the Source of All Life. It was a gift of grace that I will carry with me forever. I am not afraid of physical death for it is just a passing from a more restricted life to a more fully alive life. And yet I know it is our duty to bring into this physical life the awakened knowledge of our true life existence and bridge the worlds of conscious existence until they merge in truth to the only world that exists—the dwelling place of the Creator.

Miracles

Miracles are an extension of God's love for us. They appear in many forms and are always the result of Divine Spirit's love. They are ever-present and abundant. We do not choose miracles; they are given to us. But we can be more open to their natural occurrence and become what is now commonly called miracle-minded, which is being always ready for a miracle. For when our perception is in tune with the awareness of Divine Spirit, we become increasingly open and ready for miracles. Miracles then become the natural order of things, and we become less and less surprised by their occurence. We cease judging them as lesser or greater, for a miracle is a miracle. It is an extension of love from Creator to created. We can be a vessel for miracles of the Holy Spirit in our daily lives if we just show up and be ready for the miracles to unfold. Divine Spirit loves willingness and openness to possibility. In each moment, remember to affirm the miraculousness and beneficence of Spirit, and you will start seeing the multitude of miracles that awaits only your invitation to witness them.

So many of the healing stories I have shared with you involved miracles of physical healing, soul evolvement, and the fellowship of humans. But these are only some examples of the kinds of miracles that exist. In our daily lives there are so many opportunities to witness and receive the miraculous that one chapter or book could not possibly hold all of the miracles that are occurring in the very instant you read this line. We may naturally, in our humanness, deem some smaller or larger, but the truth, of course, is that they are all equal. There are so many miracles I see in each day when I remember to look, that to me miracles are, indeed, the natural order of our existence. Divine Spirit will eternally be what it is; it is we who are sometimes asleep or awake. I now love being awake as much as possible for the joy and love that is present for us transcends all. So give all your problems, crises, and daily life tasks and events over to Divine Spirit and ask for a miracle. You are allowed to ask and affirm the miracle-giving Spirit that exists all around and within us. You just cannot determine the nature of the miracle that comes for Spirit is oh-so-much wiser than we are. To your surprise, in retrospect Divine Presence will always have chosen rightly. When you show up and are miracle-minded, the results of love will follow.

In this vein I would like to speak briefly regarding requests to Divine Spirit in meditation, in prayer, and in miracle-asking. It is okay to let Divine Spirit know the achings and yearnings of your heart and soul. It is most natural if we or ones we love are ill or in crisis to ask for healing through divine intervention or a miracle. But it is important to affirm that Divine Mind knows best in all situations. For acknowledging that the will of God and the wisdom of God are greater and more healing for all souls than our personally invested requests is part of the evolution of our own souls. In affirming that "Thy will not mine be done" even in personal pain, suffering, or loss, you are taking a leap of faith into the hands of God. This surrender brings the compassion of Divine Spirit to your door. For if you can trust in your Higher Power and leave the little self behind, you are surely on your way to the abundance of miracles and Divine Blessings which awaits you.

You all have miracle stories in your lives. Remember one here and share it with others silently, in your prayers, through writing, art or music, or in your thoughts. The mind that remembers a miracle is a mind that remembers God. Let us all remember our miracles and share them with one another. In joined miracle-mindedness, we find the love of God.

Chapter 10

✳

THE LIFE CYCLE AS A SACRED JOURNEY

When we begin to view this physical lifetime as an opportunity to evolve our souls toward the golden truth of who we are in connection to the Divine Creator, the life cycle becomes a sacred healing journey. We begin to view, however dimly at times, the power and preciousness of the human spirit in this journey we call life, and all the events and activities in our lives become opportunities for evolving the soul and its consciousness. When we enter into a conscious spiritual commitment to self-knowledge, the spiritual gates within open and we begin to learn the mysteries of our souls. Within each of us are the glory of God and the joy of eternal life. In this present physical lifetime we can honor who we are and follow the path within us to awaken to our higher nature and become spiritually evolved and conscious beings.

This awakening is real and possible in all of our struggles and daily activities. For when the mind, soul, and spirit are focused primarily on their own divine natures in connection to their source of Divinity, all the laws of physical reality are transmuted. In every moment that one's total attention is focused on the light of the Divine, whether within oneself, in all of humanity, or in all the things of the earth, the celestial world of truth grows brighter in physical reality. The evolving soul's journey is to heal itself and all those whose lives it touches. This means that in every aspect of life, we consciously ask for and listen to Divine Guidance. There is no corner or piece of our lives that is not given to the Almighty for guidance and divine interpretation. In all things we learn to speak to Spirit and honor the Divine Mind as our source.

In the beginning of our conscious awakening we may set a time period to meditate, self-examine, or pray. Even then we may ask to remember to give all life situations and daily activities to Divine Wisdom. Through the habitual practice of conscious spiritual energy disciplines, we lay the groundwork for an ever-increasing connection to the divine spiritual energy within and without, and we progress in soul evolvement guided by the One who created us. Through all the rigors and challenges of life, we can be filled with divine life force in an awakened and conscious state. Through the perceived harshness and difficulties of physical life, we can come upon the greater truths of our spiritual oneness with the Divine. We can honor our humanness and all that we see, feel, and experience and still reach for the higher ground. We can allow ourselves healing and still know that our pain, suffering, or sadness are temporal in the higher realms of consciousness. There is no denial of human emotions and life experiences; there is just an awakening to the fact that this is not the only reality and there is a way to live life which transcends suffering and brings the peace of God.

When we attempt through our daily spiritual practices of meditation, self-examination, and prayer to evolve our souls and consciousness, we can embrace all human life experiences as part of our soul's growth and illumination. We are not perfect beings, for we are human, and yet we are given the opportunity here and now to experience the perfection of divine love during every moment in which we remember to. We can plan and practice to remember divine love more and more during our lives. We can do it daily during specific allotted time periods and then continue throughout the day to experience our conscious God-directed thoughts whenever we remember to. By actively performing spiritual energy disciplines we increase our consciousness of spiritual energy within us and awaken the soul and consciousness to all that needs to be learned. It is an ever-unfolding and marvelous journey which brings us to the place of miracles, of transformation, of soul's vibration toward greater divine manifestation, and to the truth of our very divine existence.

In the physical human journey we have spiritual purpose and divine destiny. It is utterly our own choice to awaken and develop our souls to live in this moment. We each can create a life devoted to remembering more and more often our awakened soul. In all religions there are daily prayer practices and holy days set aside as especially significant. There are days to rejoice in the beauty and abundance of God's gifts and light and there are days in which inner reflection, atonement, and forgiveness are sought. There are days of mourning and fasting. There is often one day of every week set aside for worshiping the Almighty and for spiritual disciplines. There are often weeks or passages of time that are of historical religious significance and symbolize the spiritual or religious trials and triumphs of a people. There are events of great jubilation and celebration: birth, passage into greater inner knowledge of God, and sacred long-held spiritual/religious traditions. Throughout the religious world there is a yearly cycle of celebrations marking historical events and sacred meanings. Within each religion, this framework structures the practice of the spiritual disciplines and doctrines.

The framework varies with the faith, but the common threads that join all religions are the ideas and practices of moments, days, events, and passages of spiritual significance honoring the Almighty.

In our own lives, religious or nonreligious, we can undertake to create our own calendar of awakened spiritual consciousness. We can create personal traditions for honoring Spirit in our life events and life cycles. This calendar can be joined to an established religious practice or created especially for an individual, family, or spiritual community. We can personally and consciously empower ourselves in our spiritual practices by honoring the natural course of human life. There are times of celebration, joy, and happiness. There are times of abundance and sharing. There are times of inner reflection and solitude. There are times of grief and mourning. There are atonement and self-examination. There is forgiveness. There is healing. There are both darkness and light in our lives. The honoring of our soul's journey through all these passages is possible. The daily practice of meditation, self-examination, and prayer allows the human spirit to honor each of these times. And we do so with the comfort and guidance of a Higher Power greater than ourselves and in fellowship with humanity.

When we place the development of our relationship to a Higher Power first in our lives, we cannot fail to evolve our souls. Though the course may be difficult at times, the soul prevails when it is set upon the divine within. We may deal with sickness, suffering, adversity, and despair and yet know the peace of God. During all of life's circumstances and events there is a time to be still and find the truth. In that moment of enlightenment lies all healing.

We come to the place of being still and knowing truth through our spiritual practices. In the courage to be present consciously with ourselves as we are, we grow and reach forward to those places within that need the illumination of the soul awakened in its connection to God.

This means showing up for our everday life in a God-conscious state. In all situations, from business meetings to caring for our children, we can consciously choose to be connected to Divine Light. The earth we walk upon, the people we meet or have relationships with, are all a part of the Divine Spirit. Therefore, in all of our daily experiences we can proceed in spiritual wakefulness and be open to our soul's lessons for evolvement.

The things that begin to occur when life is lived in this manner are extraordinary. We begin to find our spiritual purpose and presence. Though external circumstances may shift all around us, within there is a growing awareness of the truth of our being. Our external life will begin to reflect the inner workings of a soul joined to its purpose and truth. Life may appear chaotic at times, but that is sometimes necessary as inner shifting occurs. We may question our work in the world and all the things we have held to be important. We may begin to see all things and circumstances in a new light of consciousness.

We begin to choose those experiences that nurture our souls as the paramount experiences in our lives. The circumstances or life situations that no longer serve our divine purpose fade. We consciously begin to choose the health of our soul's illumination over that which wastes or sidetracks our healing. We find life inordinately precious and meaningful. We create space and time in our lives for the beauty of the unfolding divinity. And we plod along through some days and cosmically fly through others. We learn to hold the hands of those in need and be truly present with them in their experiences. We learn to let our hand be held when we are in need of hand-holding and to accept a hug when we need a hug: we learn of the beauty of the human spiritual experience and allow ourselves to feel the depth of emotions, love, and pain. We allow all souls their journeys whether consciously with us or on their own paths. We honor the life within us and around us and bless the path of humanity with our thoughts, prayers, and souls. And we continue to evolve and do the work of Spirit.

All of the preceding spiritual and metaphysical language for what occurs when we view the life cycle as a sacred healing journey is simply the song of the soul. In the physical reality we do our simple spiritual disciplines as regularly and often as possible to bring us to this soul evolvement and enlightenment.

Meditate before you start your day. Pray before you go to sleep. Self-examine at some point during the day. And so on and on. We practice, practice, practice to let the soul sing to us and harken our consciousness to the path. Our practices can be playful and full of joy. We can splash in the surf with our children in blissful, unencumbered joy at the feel of the water, the sand, the sun, and the love. We can delight in the movement and rhythm of dance and music that vibrate the body and enliven the soul. We can lie back in a warm bath in the candlelit glow and sigh with the comfort that our immersion in water and soft light brings while we think of God.

All the spiritual disciplines are available in all our activities and practicable in the realm of what is called the "real" world even by those who think of the spiritual worlds as unreal, or more truthfully, unattainable in the physical reality. In every aspect of physical reality, Divinity can make itself known. For Divinity is within every part of all physical reality, which would not exist without Divine Consciousness. We are human: we will forget, and we will remember. We can place practices in our lives that foster remembering.

Through all the earth years in a life cycle we can become more proficient at allowing our inner light to grow and radiate. Our personalities, with all of their hidden flaws and darkness, can begin to sparkle with the revealing and transformative power of spiritual practices. We may have many character defects or weaknesses that we can bring to the light and with the Higher Power's guidance begin to transcend them. We may have jobs or relationships that do not serve us, and learn in the course of our spiritual disciplines and the Higher Power's wisdom the ways in which to move on and embrace new life experiences. These will serve us more fully. Remember to bless the path and those who brought us on the healing journey.

In these simple spiritual energy disciplines, our souls are given the freedom and grace to soar unfettered to spiritual fulfillment. Though the path may be dark at times, there is a light and a comforting Divine Presence each and every day in any and all circumstances. Do the practices that teach you how to listen and hear the voice of truth within. Practice in prayer the joining with the Almighty. Follow the path your prayers take to the One to whom you pray. All is within you.

Daily Practices on the Sacred Healing Journey

There are endless ways to practice the energetic spiritual disciplines that bring healing and transformation to the self and to the world, and these disciplines are the most practical and efficient means for creating love and healing in our lives. We live in a world with much to be healed. Ignorance, violence, sickness, corruption, hunger— tragedies of all kinds—do exist in this physical human reality. Though most people do not recognize the real power spiritual practices have in affecting physical reality, those who are awakened do know this power. The power of minds joined to Divine Consciousness can shift the physical reality.

There are ways you can prove this to yourself in daily living. Take a circumstance that appears difficult and energetically join in thought and attention to the Divine Love that exists in that moment. You could be sitting in rush hour traffic and bring your consciousness or thoughtful awareness to the divine light that dwells in every human being in the cars around you. You can take this so-called idle and meaningless time to remember the light that radiates within all souls. Because of your meditation and prayer practices, you can actually feel the knot of anxiety in your stomach fade into the fullness and love that come from sitting in an energetically connected manner to the love of God. You will see a physical manifestation of your changed mind and spiritual activity. Whether traffic starts moving again or you arrive at your destination at the right time or you gather such calm and spiritual refreshment that nothing else really matters, you will have effected real change just by switching your mind and spirit to a spiritual realm. That is the key: remember to switch your mind.

One spiritual mind exercise that always works is sending divine light consciousness to any situation where a human is in trouble. In passing the scene of an accident where appropriate help is already present you can assist those in trouble with your spiritual practices. Join with the ever present Divine Love within and without and direct your love to those in need. Affirm and send your Higher-Powered love light to them. Miracles happen in this light.

When you begin to see the physical manifestations of conscious spiritual energy practices, what you see merely affirms the truth of our being. Spirit and mind are supreme over the physical. The physical reality is a temporary reality, a learning place and a schoolroom.

The more minds that are joined in knowing this reality, the quicker the earth and physical reality will become a truer projection of the higher worlds of celestial existence. We seek to uplift the vibrations of the entire planet and of humanity. This sounds like an awfully large undertaking, but it is not. The power exists within each soul.

Daily life can become an exciting spiritual mission. Though a task may appear impossible, with Divine Wisdom and personal soul empowerment, it can be accomplished with ease. When a clerk in a supermarket puts his love and good will energetically into every bag he packs and into every hand he touches with change or a receipt, a greater transaction occurs. The recipients of the clerk's packages may sense an inner shift or lifting of a burden, or a lightness in their steps which happens spontaneously, and they do not know why. They have just been touched by an angel of good will and light at the downtown supermarket.

We can all become angels in those moments when we remember. And we have something more powerful than the angels have—free will to choose to bring our human darkness back to the realms of light. We are, in fact, recovering the Divine Light that was lost through forgetfulness, and restoring that light to the Creator. These are sacred and holy acts. In all our good deeds, kindnesses, and courageous inner work, we are coming closer to the source of ourselves.

Let us do all of our daily activities with a spiritually conscious mind and spirit. Be open to the possibilities of Divine Love in all matters. Through daily spiritual practices, each of us becomes more like spirit. In seeking to devote our attention, time, and activities in the direction of Divine Light, we become increasingly of the Divine Light within and are able to manifest that in the physical reality we call life. With this heightened consciousness our lives become more joyous and purposeful. We can walk upon any path on earth we choose with the strength, wisdom, and courage of a Power greater than ourselves.

It is so easy and simple to begin the self-healing journey. The world is much closer today thanks to communications technology. We can open our eyes and minds to the myriad of healing/spiritual options available. We just require the willingness to try. With all of the spiritual, psychotherapeutic, and holistic health options available to us through health stores, bookstores, fellowship programs, and directories, we are living in a time of many choices and opportunities. We need only seek out that which fits. We are not limited in our choice of spiritual practice. An established religion can take on new personal meaning when joined with spiritual energy disciplines.

We can own our personal power to become whole integrated beings with control over our lives and healing. Through the practices of meditation, self-examination, and prayer, we can come to the truth of our lives and our goals. Of course life is not an easy journey. But it is a learning journey, and it can become a sacred healing journey.

We all have obligations, jobs, families, and work in the world. We have physical bodies to take care of, minds to take care of, and a human spirit to take care of. We can do all these things well with the right tools. A full and nurtured self has much to offer and chooses its tasks, activities, and relationships with discernment.

Transformation of the self and healing of the self are one and the same. Most people desire happiness, joy, and peace in their lives. Happiness is there for the taking if we will take the first step. Yes, there will be times of unsettling darkness, pain, and sadness, but there can also be a steady calm that comes from joining with a greater truth and love that will underlie all passages. This thing called a physical lifetime is a wondrous and soul-challenging journey—let us grab it and use our whole being to make the most of it.

If we live life this way—through the practice of the spiritual disciplines—we will eventually live each day and moment in a new and embracing manner. Out will go the baggage of unresolved and unworked-through past life histories; in will come truer spiritual energetic connection to oneself and Divine Consciousness. Your soul will be free to explore what it now chooses. How do we get there? Just put one foot in front of the other and do the work. So often we wish for the magical person or thing that will make everything all right. The magic is inside you—only it isn't just magic. It is real power to change. Change takes effort. It takes energy. If you don't have enough of your own energy, go out and borrow some from those who are sharing it. They are all around you. They are called therapists, mentors, healers, clergy, fellowships, friends, physicians, etc. You can learn how to harness and balance your own energy through three simple spiritual disciplines that will affect health and healing on every level of your being. Your physical body will be nurtured, your mind will be nurtured, and your soul will be nurtured. This is called healing.

And as you search for and find your healing path, you will become a healing presence to all in your life. Your relationships will become richer and more abundant with the realness of a life lived in clear and full human connection. Gone will be the superficial and false pretenses of some invented code of polite indifference. Gone will be the meaningless chatter that does not want to scratch below the surface of humankind for fear of seeing something bad. Instead we will become capable of true emotional and spiritual connection to others, for we have connected to this within ourselves. Realness happens. Our children, our loved ones, our friends, and acquaintances will have the rewards of a relationship with a grounded and self-connected human being. In seeking our own purposes and peace within, we truly have much to bring to our relationships with others.

There are too many gifts that are given to the courageous self-healing soul to enumerate. Divine Spirit recognizes each soul's special journey and brings to each that which is needed. So we will all have our unfolding miracles and revelations, our dreams that speak to our spirits and minds, our lives that change, open, and grow to reflect our own inner longing and peace. And each of us will have our own healing stories to share on the sacred journey of life.

ADDITIONAL
INFORMATION

For further information on Healers available in your area contact:

Healing Light Center
261 Alegria Avenue, Suite 2
Sierra Madre, CA 91024
(818) 306-2170

or

Joseph Sciabbarrasi, M.D.
Los Angeles Healing Arts Center
2211 Corinth Avenue, #204
Los Angeles, CA 90064
(310) 477-8151

Provides general and family medicine, acupuncture, acupressure, homeopathy, biofeedback, nutrition, and more.

BIBLIOGRAPHY

Bruyere, Rosalyn L. *Wheels of Light.* Sierra Madre, CA: Bon Productions, 1989, 1991.

Gilman, Sid and Newman, Sarah Winans. *Manter and Gatz's Essentials of Clinical Neuroanatomy and Neurophysiology.* 7th ed. Philadelphia: F. A. Davis, 1987.

INDEX

H

I

J

K

L

M